Happy Fathers Day
1994

Love, John & LeeAnne

HOW THE CADILLAC GOT ITS FINS

Also by Jack Mingo

How to Spit Nickels and Other Tricks
I Am My Own Best Casual Acquaintance
(with Brad Bunnin, under the name Shanti Goldstein)
The Whole Pop Catalog
(editor, with the Berkeley Pop Culture Project)
Prime Time Proverbs
The Couch Potato Guide to Life
The Official Couch Potato Handbook

HOW THE CADILLAC GOT ITS FINS

AND OTHER TALES FROM THE ANNALS OF BUSINESS AND MARKETING

JACK MINGO

HarperBusiness
A Division of HarperCollins*Publishers*

HarperCollins books may be purchased for educational, business, or sales promotional use. For information, please write: Special Markets Department, HarperCollins Publishers, Inc., 10 East 53rd Street, New York, NY 10022.

FIRST EDITION

Designed by Alma Hochhauser Orenstein

Library of Congress Cataloging-in-Publication Data

Mingo, Jack, 1952–
  How the Cadillac got its fins : and other tales from the annals of business and marketing / Jack Mingo. — 1st ed.
    p. cm.
  ISBN 0-88730-677-2
  1. United States—Commerce—History—Anecdotes. 2. United States—Industries—History—Anecdotes. 3. New products—United States—History—Anecdotes. 4. Marketing—United States—History—Anecdotes. 5. Businessmen—United States—Anecdotes. I. Title.
HF3021.M557   1994
338.0973—dc20   94-2392

94 95 96 97 98 ❖/HC 10 9 8 7 6 5 4 3 2 1

Contents

Introduction

When I started working on this book, a friend asked me why I was writing it. He thought a book about business, even business weirdness, "sounded boring." Then I started telling him about Jell-O, VW Bugs, Apple Computer, and MTV, and he was amazed.

It's a problem of mythology. Many people in business like to hold on to certain myths because they justify who they are and what they do. These *myths* are what's boring about business stories.

For example, one myth is that most successful business leaders are hard-working, rational people who base their decisions on measurable data and sound business practices. This myth assures us that no successful new product is possible without a lot of meetings, computer printouts, high-priced consultants, MBAs, pie charts, flow charts, market research, reports, and rational step-by-step decision making.

The *reality* is much more interesting: "Business as usual" is often the enemy of successful innovation. Despite corporate lip service about honoring innovation, nearly every genuinely new product or procedure is initially greeted with "killer phrases": "We can't do that" or "We already tried it once years ago and it didn't work" or even "Why the hell would you want to do *that*?"

The reality is that many of our most beloved products were developed by hunch, guesswork, and fanaticism, by creators who were eccentric—or even stark raving mad. That's because making something genuinely new requires a different way of looking at things. To quote a widely circulated bad attitude wall plaque: "You don't have to be crazy to work here, but it helps."

There are a lot of examples of the fine line between genius and insanity. How else to explain Dr. John Kellogg, who developed Corn Flakes to reduce the human sex drive? Or razor man King Camp Gillette, who hoped to be elected chairman of the board for the entire world? Or Robert Welch, who turned the Sugar Daddy caramel sucker into a blunt weapon against the "Illuminati conspiracy" and worldwide communist menace?

How the Cadillac Got Its Fins is dedicated to the millions of eccentrics, weirdos, kooks, and wackos on all levels who have been, and always will be, responsible for new things. Even if you're disguised in that pinstriped camouflage, we can see that telltale gleam in your eye, and we salute you.

—JACK MINGO
Alameda, California

HOW THE CADILLAC GOT ITS FINS

How Two Bad Apples Created a Computer Company

Good artists copy. Great artists steal.
—Steve Jobs, stealing a quote from Pablo Picasso

It is a hoary old tale told around Silicon Valley about how the first personal computer worthy of the name was built in a garage by two young geniuses (or one genius and an opportunist, depending on who's telling the story). And much of the story is true, although it has been somewhat elevated and amplified by the Apple PR machine.

Four years before the Apple computer, Steve Wozniak was a college student living in the student dorms of the University of California when his mom inadvertently pushed him toward a life of crime. Knowing his interest in esoteric electronics, she sent him an article from the October 1971 *Esquire* called "Secrets of the Little Blue Box." It told of an underground network of "phone phreaks," forerunners of the computer hackers of a decade later, who built "blue boxes" that allowed them to outwit the billing mechanisms of the phone company and make long distance phone calls all over the world—for free. But that was just the beginning—with the right series of beeps and boops, phone phreaks could tune in to governmental networks used by U.S. law enforcement and espionage agencies, and even AUTOVON, the military phone system.

Wozniak was so excited by the article that he stopped midway through and called his friend Steve Jobs, who was four years younger and still a sophomore in high school back in the San Jose suburb where Wozniak had grown up. The two had been friends for years, bound by a mutual interest in electronics and a certain nerdy disinterest in developing social skills that made them both semi-outcasts from their peer group.

The two Steves decided to start making blue boxes. Over the next four months, they pored over reference materials and built a tone-generating oscillator from plans in *Popular Electronics*. But it was hard to keep it tuned well enough to fool phone company equipment, so Wozniak designed a small digital device powered by a 9 volt battery.

This machine yielded more reliable tones and fooled Ma Bell! The two Steves began playing phone phreak games with the device. They called weather numbers in Australia, dial-a-prayers in Munich, and even the Vatican. They tried "tacking tandems," in which they routed a call from exchange to exchange across the world and back to the phone booth down the hall so that you could say hello, run to the other phone, and hear your own spookily echoed voice ten seconds later. But, in a foreshadowing of their future partnership, Jobs got tired of the technological games and decided it was time to make some money from his friend's invention.

Parts for the blue boxes cost forty dollars; it took Wozniak an hour to wire them together. Jobs laid out his idea: He would pay for the materials if Wozniak would do the work. They'd split the profits fifty-fifty. Wozniak agreed. Soon the two were hawking their little devices door to door in the university's male dormitories (they figured women wouldn't be interested and besides, neither Steve felt particularly comfortable approaching them). The devices then spread to Southern California through a friend who set up shop as their distributor in Beverly Hills.

The two sold more than two hundred of the boxes for $150

each. They were never caught or prosecuted. Some of their customers were, though, including convicted swindler Bernie Cornfeld and musician Ike Turner.

About a year later, the phone company refined their switching mechanisms, making the boxes obsolete.

Wozniak began the process of flunking out of college. Meanwhile, Jobs began the process of dropping out of life. He went off to college at an avant-garde campus in Oregon where he spent his first semesters using LSD and marijuana, discovering sex, and investigating Zen Buddhism, communes, and gurus. He adopted a diet from the writings of Arnold Ehret, a nineteenth-century Prussian who taught that eliminating mucus, gas, and "excessive excrement" from one's body is the key to health, happiness, and mental stability. It didn't take long before Jobs flunked out of college and moved back in with his parents.

By claiming that he had once worked at Hewlett-Packard, Jobs talked his way into a five-dollar-an-hour technician's job at Atari, maker of the first successful video game, Pong. There he managed to alienate nearly all of his coworkers by poking his nose into their work and telling them what "dumb shits" he thought they were. He was unkempt and sloppy, even by computer programmer standards, and he told people that he could go without bathing because of his vegetarian, "no-mucus" diet. His supervisor, Al Alcorn, thought otherwise. He moved Jobs to a one-man night shift, noting that "the engineers didn't like him, and he smelled funny." Night work also meant that nobody was looking over Jobs's shoulder as he worked. Good thing, too, since he wasn't a particularly brilliant worker.

He was assigned to work on engineering a game called Breakout, which was basically a Pong handball game with a wall of individual bricks that disappeared as you hit them. He tried to do the work himself, but discovered that he was in over his head, so he appealed to Wozniak to help out. Ever-trusting Wozniak agreed to do the job.

Atari paid a bonus every time a game designer was able to reduce the number of chips in a game because fewer chips resulted in less cost to the company. Nobody was better than Wozniak at using less for more results. Jobs agreed to split the bonus, which he said would be $700. "Steve wasn't able to design anything that complex," said Wozniak later. "I designed the game thinking that he was going to sell the game to Atari for $700 and that I would receive $350. It wasn't until years later that I learned that he had actually sold the game for $7,000." Jobs also soaked up the credit for the game, never telling anybody at Atari about Wozniak's work. Afterward, he took his money and disappeared for a while to an Oregon farm commune.

Meanwhile, Wozniak, living with his parents after dropping out of Berkeley, got a job at Hewlett-Packard designing calculators. But he was really interested in designing computers. He started attending the Homebrew Computer Club in Menlo Park, a group of about thirty hobbyists, engineers, programmers, and technicians who met every two weeks to talk about building small computers. This was in 1975, when computers were huge, room-sized behemoths costing enormous amounts of money that were programmed by a sequence of cards with holes punched in them. Only big universities, corporations, and governmental agencies could afford them. One goal of the Homebrew Club was to wrest the monopoly of computers away from these oppressive institutions and provide them as a tool for liberation for The People.

The early gatherings at first seemed as quixotic—considering the expense of and complexity of computing—as a group getting together to build their own spaceships.

But there was reason for hope. It was clear that microprocessors, the "brains" of computers, were getting dramatically cheaper, smaller, less complex, and more powerful. Through miniaturization, engineers had gotten the computing power of a house-size mainframe onto a chip of silicon the size of a Pez candy.

Members of the club began sharing schematics and scrounging, swapping, and selling electronic parts. (One member who started importing parts from Asia was summoned to U.S. Customs because of a box labeled "joysticks." From the name and shape of the components, the inspector thought he was smuggling some sort of exotic and probably illegal sexual device.)

Homebrew Club members quivered with excitement when the January 1975 *Popular Electronics* announced the release of the Altair 8800, the first computer kit for hobbyists. It sold for $375. But even for diehard electronics freaks, the Altair was daunting. It came without software or even an operating system, so it had to be programmed by the purchaser. It needed to be soldered together by the buyer and attached to additional memory chips and a teletype or TV screen before it would do anything vaguely interesting, pushing the actual cost up to about $3,000.

Still, the Altair suggested that computing by individuals was possible. The Homebrew Club spent a lot of time thinking about the things small computers could be used for. Manufacturers at the time thought they would mostly control machines and appliances, but the Homebrew Boys came up with a more prophetic list: Personal computers could be used to control burglar alarms, car engines, sprinklers and heating systems, to make music, edit text, play games, and make robots work.

Wozniak couldn't afford the Altair kit. Besides, just building a kit wouldn't have been a challenge. He started designing his own microcomputer, using parts that he and Jobs scrounged.

(Finding parts wherever they could was a tradition among early computer freaks. Methods included Dumpster-diving to outright theft. For example, Atari tightened up security when management discovered that it was losing an average of $800 in boards and chips *every day*.)

Wozniak's new computer wasn't actually his first. As a young teenager, he had teamed up with a friend and put together a primitive device that would multiply simple numbers. His proud mom had asked the *San Jose Mercury* to send a reporter. But when Wozniak demonstrated the device, smoke and an acrid smell poured from it as it dramatically burned out. "We didn't get our picture in the paper," recalled his disappointed friend, "and we didn't get to be boy heroes."

This time he didn't have a disaster. The computer worked exactly as he had hoped. But when he offered manufacturing rights to his bosses at Hewlett-Packard, they listened politely and turned him down, saying "HP doesn't want to be in that kind of market."

But Jobs was interested. He began badgering Wozniak about selling copies of Wozniak's circuit board as a kit for members of the Homebrew Club and other hobbyists. Jobs suggested they start their own computer company, and he even had a name picked out. He remembered his days in the orchards on the farm commune in Oregon, and also wanted a name that would appear before Atari in the phone book. He suggested the name Apple Computer.

Wozniak wanted something more technical, more serious, more in keeping with the technobabble clichés of Silicon Valley firms. Something like Executek or Matrix Electronics. Besides, he was afraid that the Beatles might take them to court because their record company was named Apple Corps. But Wozniak eventually agreed that he couldn't come up with anything any better than Apple, so that was the name they put on the paper when they signed an agreement on April Fools' Day, 1976. (It turns out that Wozniak's fears were well-founded. Twelve years later, the Beatles' company did indeed sue, claiming that the musical capabilities of the Macintosh broke a secret 1981 agreement made by Apple Computer to stay off Apple Corps' music/entertainment turf.)

To make the first hundred boards would take money. Wozniak sold his prized HP-65 calculator for $500; Jobs, not wanting to let on that he still had $5,000 in the bank from the sale of Breakout to Atari, sold his VW van to raise his half of the money.

Reaction at the Homebrew Club was muted. But one of the few members who was enthusiastic owned three small stores that catered to computer hobbyists. His name was Paul Terrell. He told Wozniak that he didn't want the circuit board, which would require assembly by the buyers—he wanted completely built computers. He was willing to buy fifty Apple I computers, cash on delivery, if they came completely assembled.

That was a windfall for the two Steves, and a burden. They had to scramble for about $25,000 in credit to assemble the parts. They set up shop in the garage of Jobs' parents' house and recruited members of the Jobs family to help, paying Steve's younger sister one dollar a board to insert capacitors and resisters into the right places. (She found she could do four boards an hour while watching soap operas and "The Gong Show.")

They finished the computers, added up their costs, and whimsically decided that the computer should cost $666.66. Terrell, however, was less than pleased at their shipment: The "computers" were bare boards without cabinets, without keyboards, without operating system software to make them run, without disk drives or any other way to load programs, and without monitors. He paid anyway and hired a cabinetmaker to build wooden cases to mount the pieces in. Nonetheless, the Apples sat collecting dust on Terrell's shelves for a long time.

Meanwhile, Wozniak started working on the Apple II. This time he was determined to make a computer so impressive it would knock the socks off the blasé Homebrew members. It would have a keyboard and built-in BASIC software. It would have sound and color so he could play his Breakout game. And it would have a lot of slots to slide new boards in so it could be expanded and updated and customized. Jobs came up with a compact molded plastic case that was a marked contrast from the squatty sheet metal cases of other minicomputers. They were now ready to take the computer world by storm. And they did.

How the Walkman Caught the World's Ear

Thank God for the Walkman. Before it, the only portable "personal stereo" was the boom box, carried on the shoulder and usually played loudly. The Walkman made it so we didn't have to be subjected to other people's questionable taste in music . . . or their whining about ours.

Best of all, the Walkman's sound is quality stereo. Nowadays, that may not seem that big a deal, but not that long ago, portable tape recorders were clunky things that played distorted music through bad speakers. If you wanted to listen privately, you had to stick a little beige plug into one of your ears; it sounded like a telephone in a tin can.

The funny thing is that the Walkman was, to the team of Sony engineers who designed it, a major disappointment. They were aiming for something completely different. Headed by Mitsuro Ida, they had earlier achieved great success with a small portable tape recorder called the Pressman. It was wonderfully compact ($5\frac{1}{4}$ by $3\frac{1}{2}$ by $1\frac{1}{8}$ inches) and included a built-in microphone and speaker. It became the standard tape recorder for journalists.

The Pressman was in mono only, and radio journalists began asking Sony for a stereo version in the same convenient size. Late in 1978, the engineers started shrinking and consolidating the components of a stereophonic tape recorder, trying to get them into the same chassis. They almost made it. They could fit in playback parts and two tiny speakers, but not the recording mechanism. Since the whole point was to come up with a recorder, the first attempt was a grave disappointment.

Still, it wasn't a bad first try. The quality of the sound was surprisingly good, considering its size, so Ida kept the prototype around the shop instead of dismantling it. Some of the engineers started playing cassettes on it while they worked on the next attempt.

Their failure weighed heavily on project leader Ida's mind. After all, Sony prided itself on its innovations in tape recorder technology. The postwar company's second product—and first success—was an innovative tape recorder that impressed the recording world in 1950. (Sony's first product, released three years earlier, was an electric rice cooker that tended to give shocks and start fires.)

One day Masaru Ibuka wandered by. He did that a lot. He was an innovator who, with Akio Morita, founded the company and was responsible for much of its early success. But, as the years went by, he was seen as too quirky and creative to fit into the smooth day-to-day operations of the corporation that Sony had become. Morita took over operations and made Ibuka honorary chairman, a ceremonial role that gave him much respect, little authority, and lots of time to wander the halls of Sony.

Ibuka watched the Pressman engineers working on their design problem. He heard music coming from the unsuccessful prototype and asked, "Where did you get this great little tape player? It sounds very nice."

Since Ibuka spent a lot of his time roaming around, he knew pretty much what was going on all over the company. He suddenly remembered another project he had looked at—a set of lightweight portable headphones that were being developed by an engineer named Yoshiyuki Kamon on the other side of the building.

"What if you got rid of the speakers and combined your stereo with his headphones?" Ibuka asked Ida. "The headphones would use less power and increase the quality of the sound. Who knows, maybe we can sell this thing even if you can't record on it. After all, it makes great music."

The engineers listened politely—while privately thinking that the old man had finally lost his bearings. Why make a tape recorder that can't record? Who would want to listen to music through headphones when they could have speakers? Why make something that would do *less* than everything that came before it? This is progress?

Ibuka, revered, honored, but with no authority to okay projects, went to his friend and partner Morita and showed him the gadget with headphones attached. Morita listened and was amazed at the quality of the stereo music. To the shock of the engineers, Morita told them to push forward with development.

The engineers were not the only ones surprised. The marketing department thought it was a terrible idea, too. They projected that the company would lose money on every unit sold. Told that the name being used in Japan, the Walkman, sounded "funny" to English ears, Sony first presented the Walkman as the Soundabout in the United States and as the Stowaway in England. The 1979 product rollout was a low-budget, lukewarm publicity affair aimed at teens.

Nothing happened. Teens are conformists, by and large, and they held back, waiting to see what their peers would do. Boom boxes continued to sell; the Walkman languished on shelves. It looked like the engineers and marketers had been right in their skepticism.

Then the yuppies discovered it. Perfect for listening to Mozart while jogging and Boy George while commuting, small enough to fit into a briefcase or the pocket of a business suit, the Walkman became a sudden, raging success among the world's white-collar class.

The Walkman's sudden fad status surprised nearly every-body at Sony—especially the hapless production manager who had been told to prepare an initial run of sixty thousand units. The number had seemed grotesquely overoptimistic, so he ordered the parts for all sixty thousand but only assembled half that number. He figured that if the Walkman sold well, he'd have enough time to begin assembling the second batch. If it didn't, he'd be a hero for saving the company money. When Walkman sales exploded and Sony was suddenly caught with bushels of orders and no inventory, the manager nearly lost his job.

Business Wisdom from the Sages

My rule always was to do the business of the day in the day.
—The Duke of Wellington, 1769–1852

No praying, it spoils business.

—Thomas Otway, 1652–1685

*Who first invented Work—and tied the free
And holy-day rejoicing spirit down
To the ever-haunting importunity
Of business, in the green fields, and the town—
To plough—loom—anvil—spade—and, oh, most sad,
To this dry drudgery of the desk's dead wood?*
—Charles Lamb, 1775–1834

No nation was ever ruined by trade.
—Benjamin Franklin, 1706–1790

He's happy who, far away from business, like the race of men of old, tills his ancestral fields with his own oxen, unbound by any interest to pay.

—Horace, 65–8 B.C.

How the Life Saver Got Its Hole

In 1913, Clarence A. Crane, a candy manufacturer in Cleveland, Ohio, was having trouble with his line. The chocolates he sold didn't travel well during the hot summer months. Candy stores would order almost nothing from him between June and September. To stay in business, he decided to develop a line of hard mints.

His factory, however, was only set up for chocolates, so he jobbed the mints out to a pill manufacturer. Unfortunately, the pill maker's machine was malfunctioning—despite all efforts, it kept punching a hole in each mint's center.

The pill manufacturer presented the first batch apologetically to Crane, and told him that they'd try to fix the problem for the next batch. Crane looked at the candy and said, "Don't bother. Keep it the way it is. They looked like little life savers!" Suddenly, he had an irresistible name for the mints.

Crane advertised his Crane's Peppermint Life Savers as a way of saving yourself from "that stormy breath." He designed a round paperboard tube and printed a label showing a crusty old seaman tossing a life preserver to a young woman swimmer. Still, he considered the product to be just a summer sideline and didn't push the idea any further.

Enter Edward John Noble, who made a living selling ad space on streetcars in New York City. One day he saw Crane's Life Savers in a candy store and bought a roll on impulse. He was so impressed with the product that he jumped on a train to Cleveland to convince Crane that he should buy streetcar ads.

"If you'd spend a little money promoting these mints," Noble told Crane, "you'd make a fortune!"

Crane wasn't interested. He still saw the mints as a sideline to his real product—chocolates. Noble persisted. Crane, to get rid of him, suggested sarcastically that he buy the Life Saver brand. He'd even throw in the defective pill machine for free. When Noble asked, "How much?" Crane was caught completely unprepared. He blurted out "Five thousand dollars."

Noble thought the price was a steal—but he didn't have that kind of money. He returned to New York and was able to raise only $3,800. He went back to Cleveland and talked Crane's down to $2,900, leaving himself with $900 for operating expenses.

Noble immediately started running into problems. It turned out that the roll Noble had tried tasted so good because it was fresh. After a week or two on the shelves, the candy started tasting like the paperboard it came in. Noble came up with a tinfoil wrapper that kept the flavor fresh, but, unfortunately, there were thousands of the old rolls sitting stale and unsold on candy store shelves. Store owners refused to order any more unless Noble exchanged the old rolls for new ones.

He made the exchanges, but the candy still wasn't selling very well. Noble started giving away free samples on street corners, to no avail. Luckily, he had kept his day job, but more and more of his weekly salary was going to propping up his company. He then came up with a brilliant marketing idea: Why sell his candy only in candy stores? He started convincing owners of drug stores, smoke shops, barber shops, restaurants, and saloons to carry Life Savers. He told them: "Put the mints near the cash register with a big 5¢ card. Be sure that every customer gets a nickel with his change, and see what happens."

It worked. With change in hand, customers impulsively

flipped a nickel back to the clerk and pocketed a pack. Noble finally began making money from his product.

Other candy manufacturers quickly discovered the magic of counter displays for impulse sales. The space around cash registers started getting overcrowded. To make sure he kept his counter space, Noble designed a large, segmented candy bin for store owners, allowing space for all the other candy products—but putting his Life Savers in the best position across the top. Life Saver counter displays can still be found next to checkout lines in supermarkets and drug stores everywhere.

Meanwhile, the company began expanding its line from the original Pep-o-mint. Life Savers became the world's best-selling candy. Since 1913, the company has sold over 44 billion of the familiar little tubular rolls.

Ben & Jerry's
Real Cool Business

Here's the scoop: Ben & Jerry's Ice Cream is a business built on a dishful of contradictions: It's a huge financial success story that came out of nonmaterial, 1960s counterculture attitudes; it's a for-profit corporation that accomplishes do-good projects that would make a nonprofit group proud; it makes a fat- and sugar-rich product that thrives among much of the same consumers who normally buy whole grain bread and low-fat Granola.

Ben & Jerry's wouldn't have happened if it hadn't been for a seventh grade gym class in 1963. Bennett Cohen and Jerry Greenfield were separately going through the shock of going to a new school at Merrick Avenue Junior High in Long Island, New York. It was a difficult transition, according to Greenfield: "We were nerds, smart kids who had no social skills. We were fat."

For fat uncoordinated kids, there are few things as humiliating as junior high PE class. Cohen and Greefield didn't know each other, but they ended up in the same class, running laps on the school track. Ben and Jerry were way at the rear. Recalled Jerry: "We were the two slowest, chubbiest guys in the class. Coach yelled, 'Gentlemen, if you don't run the mile in under seven minutes, you're going to have to do it again.' And Ben yelled back, 'Gee coach, if I don't do it under seven minutes the first time, I'm certainly not going to do it in under seven minutes the second time.' To me, this was brilliance. This was a guy I wanted to know."

The two became fast friends. They eventually learned

some social skills . . . sort of. In high school during the 1960s, when many teens were listening to loud music and experimenting with psychoactive substances and alternative lifestyles, Ben and Jerry would try to entice women to nearby Jones Beach . . . to go square dancing. With friends, they also started their own religion, grunting, growling, and dancing around a fire on the beach, sacrificing pigs' feet and imploring their god, Crux, to find them steady girlfriends. Ben was appointed editor of the yearbook, and—in a bit of real-life foreshadowing—Jerry took a job driving a truck as an after-school ice cream man.

The Vietnam War was in full swing, so college was the only safe refuge. Ben eventually got a high lottery number in the draft, so he decided it was safe to drop out and did so. Jerry, however, got a low one and stayed in Oberlin College in Ohio until he graduated, by which time the war had wound down.

After college, the two friends embarked on a string of jobs. Ben was a custodian, cab driver, bakery assistant, and pottery teacher for emotionally disturbed kids. Jerry tried unsuccessfully to get into medical school and settled for being a lab technician.

In the late 1970s, the two friends got fed up with the nondirection of their lives and decided to move to bucolic Vermont and start a business. They were open to anything, as long as it had something to do with food since, says Jerry, "We were both big into eating." They considered making bagels until they found out that the start-up costs for equipment would be in the range of $40,000. In 1978, they signed up for a five-dollar correspondence course in ice cream making from Penn State.

It changed their lives. They moved into an abandoned gas station next to the University of Vermont campus and started mixing up gallons of the stuff in an old rock-salt ice cream maker. They used all-natural ingredients (except in the Heath

Bar Crunch, packaged in an apology: "We love Heath Bars so much we couldn't help ourselves") and made a much denser ice cream than most (a gallon of theirs is about two pounds heavier than a gallon of normal ice cream, which is fluffed up with air). People flocked to their ice cream stand. Ben and Jerry made the long wait for cones more pleasant by hiring a pianist to play requests; on summer evenings they projected movies on the side of the building.

The partners began delivering hand-scooped pints around rural Vermont in (of course) a battered VW bus. By 1980, they were employing twenty people and had started wholesale distribution to stores. A *Time* magazine cover story in the early 1980s spread the word further, beginning with: "What you must understand at the outset is that Ben & Jerry's in Burlington, Vermont, makes the best ice cream in the world." Ben & Jerry's opened stores and started wholesale distribution all over the country and around the world.

The company's management policies are a refreshing whiff of patchouli in the dank and musty world of American business. For one, corporate policy dictates that the top executives can make no more than seven times the pay of the lowest paid worker. Jerry is the company's self-proclaimed Minister of Joy, trying to reduce stress and increase job enjoyment through office-time parties and games. "Any company you talk to always says, 'People are our most important asset blah blah blah blah blah,'" says Greenfield. "Yet when it comes to acting on it, you don't often see it. But I think it's becoming clearer and clearer that what's good for the people that work at your company is good for your business."

The company gives away 7.5 percent of its pre-tax profits to charities and do-good groups. An ice cream store it opened in Harlem is connected to a homeless shelter, giving jobs to its occupants and 75 percent of its profits to the shelter. To help save rain forests, the company gives 40 percent of the profits from its Rain Forest Crunch to environmental groups. Its Peace Pops raise funds for a military conversion group. It sponsors nature trails, folk music festivals, and theater groups. In its annual report, top management includes a detailed "Social Performance" section. Notes Ben: "I feel like a person has a particular set of values. My belief is that it is in the business environment that you have the most opportunity to act on those values, that we have the most potential to effect social change."

The company's open-handed policies make the founders feel good ... and it helps them sell ice cream. "Given the choice of two products of equal quality—if one does real good things with the money that's coming into it and the other is simply a faceless conglomerate—people will say 'I take this one,'" notes Ben & Jerry president Fred Lager.

"To me, the business sort of exists not really to make ice cream," says Jerry. "The business for Ben is a vehicle for social change, to make the world more equitable and just and fair. So together we have this vision of doing great things in a fun way."

How the Cadillac Got Its Fins

The 1950s era was a time of unprecedented affluence for most Americans. The Depression was over, the war was over, and after decades of doing without, Americans went on a binge, getting drunk on a cornucopia of newly available consumer things such as televisions, big refrigerators, dishwashers, hi-fi phonographs, and houses in the suburbs.

After the war, the auto companies had expanded rapidly to meet the huge demand for new cars. But, by the middle of the 1950s, demand started declining. That wasn't surprising, because almost every family that could afford a new car had bought one in the first part of the decade. The cars hadn't had time to wear out yet, and why would anyone with a perfectly good car want to go out and buy another?

Auto executives nervously watched as their market got increasingly saturated and sales began going down. What were they going to do?

They came up with something called "dynamic obsolescence," a phrase coined by chief General Motors car designer Harley Earl. It meant putting pressure on consumers to keep replacing their cars year after year—not because they didn't work any more, but because they had gone out of style. The goal of General Motors, and therefore of all American automakers, was to design cars that would look irresistible this year—and patently stale this time next year. As GM president Charles Kettering put it, "The simplest way to assure sales is to keep changing the product—the market for new things is indefinitely elastic. One of the fundamental purposes of advertising, styling, and research is to foster a healthy dissatisfaction."

A car would be designed, observed Ford designer George Walker at the time, "but right away we would have to bury it and start another. We design a car and the minute it's done, we hate it—we've got to go do another one. We design a car to make a man unhappy with his 1957 Ford along about the end of 1958."

Because so many company resources went toward cosmetic changes, engineering and other genuine advancements took a back seat in the process. The only real engineering advance in the 1950s, the high-compression engine, was developed because it gave cars enough extra power to allow designers to pile on even more accessories, more weight, and lots of extra metal at both ends.

Nobody could pile on the extra metal better than designer Harley Earl, head of General Motors' Art and Color Section. Earl had been discovered by GM executives in 1927 in Hollywood, where he had been one of the first automobile customizers, taking standard cars and making them lower, longer, and more sporty for movie stars. His trademark was to make cars look like they were moving fast—even when they were standing still. He replaced the boxy lines of the 1920s with sleek curves and angles. "My sense of proportion tells me that oblongs are more attractive than squares," he wrote, "just as a ranch house is more attractive than a three-story flat-roofed house or a greyhound is more attractive than a bulldog."

Earl carefully cultivated the image of an eccentric genius in the button-down corporate culture of GM. He dressed in unusual styles—for instance, a dark blue shirt with a white suit, neatly reversing the colors of the GM corporate uniform. He reportedly had a duplicate of every suit he owned stashed in his office closet so that he could change by midday if his clothes became rumpled.

Many of his employees also thought of him as something of a tyrant and power freak. He didn't wear the glasses he needed because he thought it diluted his authority. At six foot six inches, he towered over his staff; rumor had it that he would not hire anybody anywhere near his height, so that he would always be taller than his subordinates. Earl liked to show who was boss; surrounded by a claque of yesmen, he would quietly come up behind a designer at work and say something casual like, "Don't you fellows agree that it would look a lot better if we raised the back end of this one one thirty-second of an inch?"—an imperceptible change that ultimately resulted in many tedious hours of extra work for the designer.

Earl had always liked the look of airplanes and sometimes hung around airfields. One day during World War II, he managed to get a distant and fleeting look at a top-secret experimental airplane, the Lockheed P-38 Lightning. It had three fuselages—the middle one containing the pilot, the outside two carrying engines and fuel tanks—each of which had a tall vertical tail. When the war ended, Earl remembered the design and sketched it out for his design crew. They cautiously incorporated a small, rounded fin into the design of the 1948 Cadillac.

At first, reaction to the fin was mixed. Many people thought that even this understated fin looked funny. Earl didn't care. He knew that given enough time and advertising, consumers would not only get used to them, but actually begin seeing them as a mark of status and luxury. Over the next few years, the Cadillac's fins got a little bigger and sharper. Finally, when jet airplanes captured the public's imagination in the early 1950s, Earl decided to take it to the next step of design. He was looking through a newspaper in 1953 and saw just what he was looking for: a photo of a new jet, the Douglas F-4D Skyray. He ripped it out and put it in his pocket.

The Skyray had a delta-wing and looked a lot like a manta ray from the top and bottom. From the side or front, though, all you could see were a sharp, thin body, two wide wings, and big oblong air intakes. In 1953, the Skyray briefly held the world speed record. Earl showed the photo to his designers. The new Cadillacs were going to be angular like jets and rockets, he said, no longer rounded like locomotives and ships.

From that point every new model year brought Cadillac fins that were higher and more pointed. The fins also moved into the other GM lines . . . and became a symbol of status and luxury. Other car companies began competing with GM to see who could make the highest, widest, most flamboyant rear ends.

But not everybody was smitten with the fin craze. "What do these things do, anyway?" Soviet leader Nikita Khrushchev asked scornfully. In a 1955 speech to the Society of Automobile Engineers, pioneer industrial designer Raymond Loewy called the new cars "jukeboxes on wheels" and asked, "Is it responsible to camouflage one of America's most remarkable machines as a piece of gaudy merchandise? Form, which should be the clean-cut expression of mechanical excellence, has become sensuous and organic." A Methodist bishop thundered: "Who are the madmen who built cars so long they cannot be parked and are hard to turn at corners, vehicles with hideous tail fins, full of gadgets and covered with chrome, so low that an average human being has to crawl in the doors and so powerful that no man dare use the horsepower available?"

"Take all the fins off and you have a piece of soap with wheels on it," defended Ford styling executive Robert H. McGuire in 1958. "Those fins finish off the metal. They give full length to the car." Harley Earl was more frank in conversations with associates: "Listen, I'd put smokestacks right in the middle of the sons of bitches if I thought I could sell more cars."

The fins, in all their glorious absurdity, peaked in 1959. By the early 1960s, they disappeared completely from new cars.

The emphasis on style over substance they represented served Detroit well for the short term, but ultimately helped lead to its decline. For the sake of style, gimmicks, and "living room comfort," the average family car gained a foot and a half in length and a full half-ton in weight in the decade after 1955, while its gas mileage plunged from twenty miles a gallon to twelve. (One joke of the day had a gas station attendant telling a Cadillac owner, "Shut off your motor! You're burning it faster than I can pump it in!")

Engineering, safety, and gas mileage were given short shrift. Safety glass, seatbelts, airbags, higher gas mileage, and emissions standards were bitterly resisted. "Will this sell more cars? Will it look prettier, will it give us more horsepower? If not, we're not interested," an auto executive was quoted as saying in response to antipollution pleas from a Los Angeles County supervisor.

This knee-jerk arrogance ultimately led to mandates from the government that carmakers clean up their safety and pollution act—or else. More ominously, while Detroit fiddled with fins, contours, colors, and chrome, well-engineered cars from overseas gradually began moving into the American market.

Business Sense

What use would this company make of an electrical toy?
—Carl Orton, president of Western Union, to Alexander
Graham Bell, who offered all rights to the telephone for
$100,000

Nothing has come along that can beat the horse and buggy.
—Chauncey DePew, president of the New York Central
Railroad, warning his nephew against investing in
Henry Ford's new company

I think there is a world market for about five computers.
—Thomas J. Watson, founder, IBM

Face it, Louis. Civil War pictures have never made a dime.
—Irving Thalberg, MGM producer, advising his boss Louis
B. Mayer against buying the rights to *Gone With the Wind*

The Rise and Fall of the Sears Catalog

The Sears Wish Book was, for nearly a hundred years, a source of wonder, inspiration, entertainment, and economic populism. It destroyed the monopoly of local merchants, improving the quality of products and lowering their prices. It helped the thousands of small manufacturers who supplied it improve their products and get a national market. It brought a world of merchandise literally to the front doors of thousands of isolated farmers and villagers. During World War I, it was sent to injured doughboys in hospital to lift their spirits and remind them of what they were fighting for. During the Cold War, it was even smuggled into the Soviet Union by intelligence agencies to show the blessings of capitalism. "Two innocent articles of American life—the Sears, Roebuck catalog and the phonograph record—are the most powerful pieces of propaganda we have in Russia," commented a chief of the Associated Press' Moscow bureau. "The catalog comes first."

Luckily, the Cold War is over—neither of our best propaganda weapons exists any more.

The Sears Catalog started with Richard Sears. When he was a teen in the 1870s, Sears trained as a telegrapher to support his mother, sisters, and ill father. After his father died, Sears went through several railroad jobs, eventually becoming a station agent in North Redwood, Minnesota. Sears found that the job of station agent in a sleepy little hamlet wasn't a particularly lucrative or time-consuming job, so he began selling lumber and coal on the side.

One day in 1886, a jewelry company mistakenly shipped

some gold-filled watches to a local jeweler, who refused delivery. Before sending them back, Sears took a look at them. They looked pretty good, and the price was cheap. Sears decided to buy them himself. He got on the telegraph and tapped out a message offering the watches at a reduced price to station agents up and down the line. He quickly sold all the watches at a good profit in what was quite possibly the first successful telemarketing pitch in history.

He not only decided to order more of the watches, he decided to start his own company—the R.W. Sears Watch Company, which he took with him when he moved a year later to Chicago. He placed an advertisement in the *Chicago Daily News* classified ad section. "WANTED: Watchmaker with reference who can furnish tools. State age, experience, and salary required. Address T39, *Daily News*."

Hoosier Alvah C. Roebuck saw the ad and brought a sample of his watchmaking skills. Sears hired him for a salary of $3.50 a week plus room and board. Sears sold his watches through express agents and by mail, offering an installment plan and advertising extensively in rural papers. He made so much money that he retired in 1889 at the age of twenty-five and moved back to Minneapolis.

His retirement didn't last long. He got bored and teamed up with Roebuck again to start selling jewelry, watches, and sewing machines under the name of the Warren Company. Two years later, he decided to retire again and sold his holdings to Roebuck.

This retirement was even shorter than the first one. Sears waited one week before buying back half-interest in the company. In 1893, the partners changed the name of the company to Sears, Roebuck and Company and began expanding its line to just about anything: shoes, stoves, fishing tackle, suits and dresses, patent medicines, furniture and furnishings, beehives, cream separators, and even a "Stradivarius model violin" (bargain priced at $6.10). That year, their sales reached $388,000. Two years later, their volume was $750,000 and the Sears catalog, 538 pages long, was already becoming an institution in rural America. (In more ways than just commerce, too: for example, pages from outdated catalogs were placed in outhouses in those pre-tissue days. Not only that, many an adolescent boy found his first tantalizing glimpse into the forbidden mysteries of womanhood in its undergarment ads.)

It was a time when most farm towns had only one general store at which locals could shop. As a result, the prices that customers paid for often inferior merchandise were substantially marked up, leading first to individual grumbling and then organized protests movements like the 800,000 member semisecret society called "The National Grange of the Patrons of Husbandry," which railed against the retailers and other "gouging middlemen" who paid suppliers pennies for their products and then charged dollars for them.

Because Sears bought materials in large quantities and got volume discounts from manufacturers and shippers, the Sears catalog became a welcome alternative to high-priced local monopolies. The 1895 Sears catalog proclaimed, "We are Waging War Against Combinations, Associations, Trusts, and High-Priced Products." Populist Georgia governor Eugene Talmadge, understanding how important Sears had become to local farmers, used to end his campaign speech with "Don't trust nobody but God Almighty, Sears, Roebuck, and Eugene Talmadge."

The local merchants struck back, boycotting papers that ran advertising for Sears and the older but smaller mail-order house, Montgomery Ward. They spread the rumor that Richard Sears and Alvah Roebuck were "niggers." When Chicago clothing manufacturer Julius Rosenwald bought into

Sears, they disseminated anti-Semitic hate stories. Small-town storekeepers organized public bonfires and paid children a dime for every Sears or Ward catalog they brought for burning.

The year 1895 was a pivotal one for Sears. Besides Rosenwald's entry, there was Alvah Roebuck's exit. He said he was retiring for health reasons, but in reality, it was for sanity's sake—Richard Sears and his disorganized and reprehensibly nonchalant methods of handling suppliers and customers was driving him crazy. Sears wrote such imaginative catalog copy (he was once called the P.T. Barnum of the mail-order business) that the products didn't always live up to the promises he made. Furthermore, Sears created and tolerated a completely disorganized order-fulfillment process in which delays of thirty, sixty, sometimes even 120 days were not uncommon.

And even when filled, orders were often incorrect, putting the customer through the maddening process of waiting forever for his new butter churn and then finally receiving a baby buggy instead. Roebuck got tired of reading complaints from customers like this one: "For heaven's sake, quit sending me sewing machines. Every time I go to the station I find another one there. You have shipped me five already."

Unlike his partner, Roebuck managed to make his retirement stick for several decades, even though the company still retained his name. It wasn't until the 1930s that Sears hired Roebuck to travel around the country as a goodwill ambassador, drawing crowds of people who wanted to shake his hand and say hello.

In the meantime, new partner Rosenwald went to work. He toned down the claims of Richard Sears's catalog copy to keep it this side of consumer fraud. He instituted a quality-control and testing department to upgrade the products that the catalog offered. He doubled the number of products in the 1895 catalog and printed ordering instructions in Swedish and German for the new immigrants, including the heartwarmingly inclusive message, "Tell us what you want in your own way, written in any language, no matter whether good or poor writing, and the goods will be promptly sent to you."

Most importantly, Rosenwald began streamlining the order fulfillment department, introducing a time-schedule system in which each arriving order was given a specific time to be shipped. The goal was to get everything in the appropriate bin in the merchandise-assembly room at the preassigned time. To make this happen, the entire order department and all its warehouse space was linked together with a Rube Goldbergian system of conveyor belts, chutes, and rollers. The system made Sears ten times more efficient, according to one study, and became famous in the business world as an example of the new efficiency. Henry Ford even reportedly paid a visit while designing his pioneering auto assembly line.

Sears didn't open retail stores until 1925, when Ford's revolution made it easy for rural folks to jump in their cars and drive to the closest city to shop, putting a big dent in Sears's catalog sales. In 1931, the company diversified into insurance with Allstate. In 1973, it opened the tallest building in the world, the 110-story Sears Tower in Chicago.

In the 1980s, the company lurched away from its retailing roots and decided to become a financial institution instead. In a microcosm of what went wrong with America's economy, Sears decided providing goods and services was passé; instead, it would be really neat to make money by shuffling pieces of paper around. It bought Dean Witter and opened Financial Network Centers in its stores. In 1985, it issued its Discover credit card, which, after years of heavy advertising, has almost managed to achieve the status of "also-ran" in the credit field.

Meanwhile, its urban stores went downhill. Many were

closed, often with little or no notice to faithful customers and employees. The 1980s were a gold mine for most mail-order retailers and thousands of new catalogs appeared. Yet, ironically, Sears was unable to figure out a way to make a profit in mail order. In his time, Richard Sears had dealt with problems by coming up with innovative solutions. For example, when he needed to dramatically expand his mailing list, he wrote to his best customers asking each to distribute catalogs to twenty-four friends, relatives, and neighbors. In return, the customers received points whenever one of their chain of acquaintances sent in an order. These points could be saved and turned in for stoves, bicycles, or sewing machines. As a result, Sears catalog shopping leaped to an all-time high.

But no such solutions came to the Sears Catalog Division in our time. In 1992, the company announced that it was discontinuing its catalog. Writer Nicholas von Hoffman wrote the epitaph:

> No single social organization, of whatever character, has made a larger contribution to the nation's material welfare. The company's magnificent past makes its lousy present so much more saddening. Its record in recent years qualifies Sears to be an example of the failures of American enterprise. [It was] another company which had everything—capital, advantageous real estate, a seasoned organization, thousands of suppliers, and millions of customers rooting for it, everything that is, but an able management. . . . A measure of Sears' ever-deepening drop is that in an era when the catalog mail-order business went crazy trying to find new markets and customers, Sears, Roebuck, of all places, couldn't find a way to make its catalog division profitable.

How the Big Mac Became the Hottest Thing Between Buns

Judging by its popularity, you would think that the Big Mac was the result of sophisticated marketing by a savvy management team. Yet it wasn't that way at all. First of all, it was an idea "borrowed" from another restaurant chain. And, when it ended up on McDonald's menu in 1968, it wasn't *because* of the company's top management, but *despite* it.

In the early 1950s, the McDonald brothers of San Bernardino, California, created the first genuine fast food restaurant. They came up with an assembly line formula that they called the Speedy Service System, dishing out low-cost burgers, fries, and shakes in a fraction of the time of most drive-ins.

When entrepreneur Ray Kroc began franchising McDonald's outlets a few years later, he refined the Speedy System further, making it even more regimented. Each worker was assigned only one function, which worked out fine because the menu featured only a few items. He hired only team-oriented, college-aged men, and dressed them in white army-style uniforms. (Kroc wouldn't have women workers for more than a decade because he was afraid their presence would disrupt the operation's militarylike efficiency and attract loitering male admirers. When McDonald's finally stopped this blatant gender discrimination in 1968, the unwritten directive at the time was to hire only "flat-chested, unattractive women.")

Unfortunately, the extreme efficiency was a curse as well as a blessing. It forced Kroc to resist adding any new menu items, for fear they would slow down the system. Instead, he concentrated on perfecting the products he had, spending, for example, over $3 million to research the secret of consistently perfect french fries. After a while, customers naturally started getting tired of the same old thing every time, and McDonald's profits began leveling off. McDonald's franchisees began griping— loudly—about the lack of variety.

Kroc tried his best. He test-marketed a series of new products that he thought could be fit into the Speedy Service System. Unfortunately, he didn't have the same genius for developing new products that he did for selling franchises. All of his new products were disasters. For example, he decided in the late 1950s that the menu needed a dessert. He tried selling brownies and strawberry shortcake. When they failed to sell, he tried miniature pound cakes at fifteen cents a loaf. Nobody bought them. In desperation, he tried offering kolacky, a Bohemian pastry his mom used to bake for him. No luck.

Frustrated, Kroc gave up on desserts. He decided that what McDonald's *really* needed was a nonmeat burger for Catholics on Fridays. He went into the kitchen and concocted a product that he called a "Hulaburger": two slices of cheese and a grilled pineapple ring on a toasted bun. Not surprisingly, it bombed, and was finally replaced with a fish sandwich.

For the next decade, Kroc would fly into a rage whenever franchisees suggested new menu items. Finally, a desperate franchisee willing to risk Kroc's wrath introduced McDonald's most popular product.

Jim Delligatti was one of Kroc's earliest franchise holders. He operated a dozen stores in and around Pittsburgh. When he noticed his customer base was dwindling, he began lobbying McDonald's managers to allow him to broaden the menu.

His idea? He wanted to sell a double-decker hamburger

with "special sauce" and all the trimmings—an idea that he unabashedly stole from the Big Boy hamburger chain. He badgered Kroc until he received reluctant permission in 1967 to test-market what was to become the Big Mac. Kroc forced some conditions. Delligatti had to agree that the product would be offered in only one marginal suburban store. He also had to promise to use the standard McDonald's patty and bun—a promise he quickly reneged on when it became clear that the standard bun was too small, making the sandwich impossible to eat without its falling to pieces. He quietly ordered oversized sesame seed buns from an independent baker and had them sliced into thirds.

Within a few months, the new Big Mac had increased his store's sales volume by a healthy 12 percent. He started serving it in his other stores. Other franchisees saw what was happening and began clamoring for their own Big Macs. McDonald's quickly tried the Big Mac in other test markets. It found that the Big Mac increased sales by at least 10 percent in each test market. At the end of 1968, the Big Mac was put into nationwide distribution.

The commercials that McDonald's created featured a recital of the Big Mac's ingredients. Max Cooper, a retired McDonald's publicist who owned several franchises in Birmingham, Alabama, thought they were boring and ineffectual. So he took matters into his own hands and held a contest in his stores: Anyone who could correctly recite the ingredients of the Big Mac in four seconds got one free. An ad agency recorded his customers' attempts at "two all-beef patties special sauce lettuce cheese pickles onions on a sesame seed bun" and eventually produced radio spots using botched recitals by real customers.

The ads were an instant hit in Birmingham. Within weeks, radio stations were cosponsoring "recite the Big Mac" contests. School kids all over town practiced the slogan at home and recess. Sales of Big Macs soared 25 percent. Other franchises in the South picked up on the idea. Finally, McDonald's national marketing department took notice and spread the same strategy nationwide.

The Big Mac's success opened a floodgate of innovation among franchise holders. In 1969, Litton Cochran in Knoxville got permission to try a variation on the deep-fried apple pie his mother used to make for him. His idea was a success and spread to the national menu.

Another franchise holder discovered that customers wouldn't normally buy two orders of fries, but that nearly half would buy a double order if it were disguised as a single order. Thus was born the now popular Large Fries, offering 60 percent more product for 75 percent more money. Another franchisee invented the McDLT. Still another came up with the Egg McMuffin, ensuring McDonald's domination of breakfast sales among fast-food restaurants for many years to come.

MTV: How Video Killed the Radio Star

"I want my MTV!" With that slogan, dutifully chanted by rock stars in MTV's numerous self-promotions and by rock fans (really) to their cable companies, MTV spread quickly across the country and then the world.

MTV wasn't the rock video show on TV. It wasn't even the first all-rock cable channel. (A channel called Video Concert Hall had come and gone a few years earlier.) But it was the first to reach most of the country and much of the world—and, most importantly, actually make a profit.

The early 1980s was a conservative time. Even musicians and record companies were affected. With post-punk, post-disco, post-*everything*, the music seemed to have lost its vitality and rebelliousness. The old groups like the Rolling Stones seemed to record the same album over and over again; the new groups aspired to become old groups.

But the music product, available on those quaint LP things, was still profitable no matter how vacant it became. Which is why two absurdly unrelated corporate giants got together to squeeze a little more out of its bloated corpse. One partner was Warner Communications, parent to Warner Brothers Records. The other was American Express, which was as close to the music industry as a traveler's check is to a sound check.

They had teamed up in 1979 to finance Warner Cable, which operated cable TV systems and generated new channels. Robert Pittman had been hired to create a twenty-four-hour movie channel, which they called, oddly enough, the Movie Channel, a commercial-free premium channel. After it became a success, Pittman was given the responsibility of coming up with the company's first advertiser-sponsored channel. Pittman knew it wasn't going to be easy. Few national advertisers were interested in cable channels because they produced such a small number of viewers compared to the networks.

Pittman put together a development team that decided the key to success was an extremely well-defined viewership. Teens and young adults were an obvious choice because they were a difficult audience to reach on TV, yet were very desirable to advertisers because of their high level of disposable income.

What would bring the teens and twentysomethings? Rock music, of course, and a certain "attitude." The team began working on the technical details of a music video channel: How to get stereo through the cable channels, how to get the record companies and unions to cooperate, and whether to have video hosts (later dubbed "veejays").

In about a year, Pittman presented their proposal to the Warner Cable board of directors. The board, figuring the channel would never make money, turned them down.

Pittman believed in the idea. He arranged a last-ditch meeting with Steve Ross, head of Warner Communications, and Jim Robinson, his counterpart at American Express. After a grueling meeting, where Pittman presented videos, audience research, programming plans, and projected earnings, Robinson turned to Ross and said "Okay, I'm in for our half." Ross agreed, and the music channel was on.

The team started working on the basic assumptions of the service. A key one was that the channel would not grow old with its audience. "We accepted the fact that viewers would grow out of MTV and new viewers would grow into it," observed Pittman later. "We laid as our cornerstone the concept of 'change for change's sake.' We would change before the audience was ready for us to change." The team decided that the station would be a failure if it ever looked as if it belonged to an older generation, or even if it looked like forty and fifty year olds could understand or enjoy it.

Pittman had planned to roll out the channel in late 1981, but he heard chilling news that made him push the date forward. The record companies were cutting costs, and many were planning to phase out rock videos. Industry consensus seemed to be that the videos had only a negligible effect on record sales.

The team decided they had better start broadcasting in the summer, before the record companies completed their 1982 budgets. That didn't give them much time, considering they hadn't decided on all the basics yet . . . like what the channel would be called. Pittman liked TV-1, but that name was already trademarked by somebody else. Pittman's second choice was TV-M—Television Music. But during one late-night session programming director Steve Casey suddenly, out of the blue, piped in with "Don't you think MTV sounds better than TV-M?"

They sent the name out to several designers for ideas. One that they liked came back from a small shop called Manhattan Design: a big "M" with "TV" spray-painted across it. It became the channel's official logo. Manhattan Design's payment for the design was $1,000.

Meanwhile, MTV staffers started rounding up videos to show. Pittman began lugging presentation charts and graphs around to record companies to pitch the new channel. He promised them that MTV would identify song titles, groups, and labels at the beginning and end of all songs (failure to do this on radio was and is a pet peeve of record execs). After his presentation, most record companies agreed to provide copies of their videos, figuring it couldn't do any harm (although MCA and PolyGram flatly refused).

On opening day, MTV vaults had a grand total of only 250 videos. And it wasn't a particularly diverse selection—for example, thirty of them starred Rod Stewart. It was a gamble, but they figured that if the channel was a success, record companies would quickly come forth with more videos.

On August 1, 1981, MTV launched itself with a song called "Video Killed the Radio Star" by the Buggles (ironically, this not particularly videogenic group quickly became the victim of its own prophecy).

The fledgling channel didn't get as many cable systems to sign up as they had hoped, and lost $50 million in its start-up years—about $40 million more than they expected. To get better coverage across the country, they ran an "I want my MTV!" campaign with cameos by rock stars. It was a huge success—thousands of people actually screamed the phrase into the phone to recalcitrant cable systems—and MTV quickly spread throughout the country. By December 1984, the channel had moved into the black.

Its influence spread, too. No longer was it enough to be a mere singer or musician to make it in the world of rock—you had to have a videogenic face as well. "The MTV Look" became a cliché used in dozens of movies, TV shows, and commercials, and was eventually parodied in everything from *Naked Gun* to "Sesame Street."

The channel ran into controversy along the way. Feminists and evangelicals didn't like the half-naked women in chains that became an MTV staple. There was also a dearth of nonwhite performers. Of the sixty videos in rotation during February 1983, only two featured blacks: one by Tina Turner, the other by the multiracial group English Beat. That same year, MTV refused to play "Billie Jean" or anything else by Michael Jackson, with Pittman responding to critics that Jackson's "rhythm and blues" had no more place on MTV than country music.

Reports at the time had it that CBS then issued an ultimatum: Play "Billie Jean" or kiss our videos goodbye. Whether true or not, the song was added to MTV's playlist—and became a huge hit. MTV learned its lesson. Four years later, MTV debuted "Yo! MTV Raps" and is credited—or blamed—with spreading rap out of its deep-urban strongholds and into the suburbs. In 1990, MTV started its "Unplugged" series, featuring rock stars playing acoustic instruments. And, in 1993, its hip/moronic "Beavis and Butt-head" series was blamed for inspiring arson and animal cruelty.

Pittman left MTV in 1986, about the time it was sold to the giant cable company, Viacom, for $511 million. MTV is now a big moneymaker, wired into hundreds of millions of homes in nearly a hundred countries worldwide.

What's in a Name?

• When Cheerios came out in 1941, they were called Cheery Oats. But in 1946, Quaker Oats threatened to sue, claiming that it had exclusive trademark rights to the name "Oats." General Mills changed the name to Cheerios.

• *Fritos* corn chips were named by ice cream salesman Elmer Doolin. He stopped in a Mexican restaurant and started eating tortilla chips for the first time. He liked them so much that he bought the factory from the owner. He named the chips Fritos—Spanish for "fried."

• Borden's *Haagen-Däzs* and Kraft's *Früsen-Gladje* are artifacts of the 1980s, when people were led to believe that imported beer, cars, and ice cream are better than domestic ones. Both made-in-America ice creams were given names that are to be found in no known language. They do, however, sound vaguely Scandinavian . . . possibly the first known case of "artificially Swedened" ice cream.

• In a similar impulse, the name *Atari* was chosen so that people would think the company was Japanese.

• Would it surprise you to know that *Chun King* isn't really Chinese? The company was founded by an Italian-American named Jeno Paulucci in mostly Scandinavian-American Duluth, Minnesota.

• *Kool-Aid* was originally named Kool-Ade until bureaucrats in the Food and Drug Administration banned the use of "ade" because it means "a drink made from . . . " (take note,

Gatorade!). In response, inventor E. E. Perkins simply changed the spelling to "aid," meaning "help."

• *Fig Newtons* were invented in Cambridgeport, Massachusetts. The plant manager, to make it easier to keep track of as-yet-unnamed products, gave each of them a temporary name chosen from nearby towns. One neighboring town is Newton, and his makeshift name for the new fig cookie eventually stuck.

• *Alpha-Beta* food stores were among the first self-service groceries. To make it easy to find things, the company shelved all of their stock alphabetically. The system was quickly changed because some of the juxtapositions were discomforting, like ant poison and asparagus, but the name lived on.

• *The Gap* stores were named that in the hopes that their clothes would be able to bridge (ready for a 1960s flashback) "the Generation Gap."

• *Sony, Kodak*, and *Exxon* were all coined for the same reason: They are easy to say and remember and are not closely related to any words in any known language.

How Jell-O Got the Shakes

It wiggles. It's colorful. It's served to patients by the finest hospitals in the world. Even the Smithsonian has done a retrospective exhibit and seminar tracing its history. Like bowling and Cheez Whiz, it's so déclassé that it's hip. We're talking Jell-O, the salad that has no vegetables, the only pork product you can eat that's certified as kosher. (Gelatin is so transformed from its original forms that rabbis have ruled it not only kosher, but pareve—neither meat nor dairy.)

Gelatin appeared in Europe centuries ago (history records that Napoleon ate it with Josephine). A specialized kind, isinglass, was milky colored and made from the air bladders of sturgeons.

Modern-style powdered gelatin was developed by the American engineer Peter Cooper, founder of the Cooper Union for the Advancement of Science and Art, who also designed and built the Tom Thumb locomotive. In 1845, he patented the process of turning animal skin, bone, and connective tissue into a highly refined, flavorless, wiggly, clear material.

Unfortunately, Cooper never quite figured out how to make a silk purse out of his sow's ear creation. His gelatin never became a commercial success. Maybe it was because he just didn't have a promoter's sense for selling the wiggle and not the steak by-products: His advertisements described gelatin as "a transparent substance containing all the ingredients fitting it for table use in portable form, and requiring only the addition of hot water to dissolve it."

Cooper's product sat jiggling but dormant for a half-century, until 1895, when all things came to a man improbably named Pearl B. Wait. Wait was a maker of patent medicines and corn plasters in LeRoy, New York. One of his most successful products was a cough syrup, so he knew something about using flavors and colors to mask the unpleasant qualities of a product.

Wait had a neighbor who was also an inventor and who had an unlikely name, too. Orator Woodward's first invention was a pesticide-laced cement egg you could place in a chicken's nest to kill lice. However, he had more success marketing a coffee-substitute grain beverage called Grain-O.

The "-O" ending was a commercial fad at the time, similar to "-a-Rama" in the 1950s, or unrecognizable techno-gibberish names in the 1990s. May Wait, Pearl's wife, was inspired by Woodward's Grain-O when she named the powdered dessert mix Jell-O.

In a Hollywood treatment of the story, Wait's fruit-flavored, brightly colored gelatin would quickly become the hit of every church potluck and picnic in LeRoy. But in real life, Wait had a devil of a time getting anybody to try it, much less buy it. Finally, in disgust, he offered to sell the whole business to Woodward for $450.

Woodward bought, figuring he could use the same manufacturing and distribution system he had already set up for Grain-O. But he quickly found that no matter how good your system is, it doesn't do much good if nobody wants your product. Packages of Jell-O piled up unsold in his warehouse. One day he was walking with his warehouse superintendent, A. S. Nico, and impulsively offered to sell him the entire Jell-O business for $35. Nico looked at him, looked at the pile of unsold goods—and refused the offer.

Nico soon had reason to regret the decision. Jell-O started finding its market. By 1902, Woodward was selling $250,000 worth of the stuff a year. He started advertising, using pictures of famous actresses and opera singers serving the delicate dessert from fluted glassware on silver trays. He hired famous artists like Maxfield Parrish and Norman Rockwell to illustrate his advertisements and recipe books. He began direct-mail ad campaigns, sending recipes directly to the consumer, and sent out a fleet of nattily dressed salesmen to appear at country fairs and women's clubs and demonstrate the ease and versatility of Jell-O.

Jell-O advertised heavily on radio and sponsored Jack Benny's show in the 1930s, but the true Golden Age of Jell-O came in the 1950s. Its ease of preparation and versatility of use in recipes brought forth the collective creative genius of American housewifery. On file at Jell-O headquarters are over 2,200 different Jell-O recipes. They range from *Joy of Jell-O Cookbook* favorites like Gelatin Poke Cake to new wave Jell-O recipes like Primordial Aspic (green Jell-O with gummy fishes and worms suspended in it). General Foods, which owns the brand, maintains an active hotline for recipes, questions, and even Jell-O wisdom (for example, did you know that there are certain fruits like pineapple, kiwi, papaya, and mangoes that should only be used canned? Canning destroys an enzyme in them that keeps the Jell-O from fully hardening).

Jell-O started falling from its slippery state of grace in the 1960s. Part of it was general antiestablishmentarianism, part was a health-consciousness backlash against artificial ingredients and empty calories, and part had to do with the baby bust. Jell-O became a punch line signaling a lower-class mentality in jokes by people like Archie Bunker and Fred Sanford. Jell-O's sales declined precipitously from a high of 715 million packages in 1968 to 305 million by 1986.

But Jell-O started bouncing back in 1987, thanks to the 1980s Baby Boomlet. Jigglers, a high-density finger-food Jell-

O recipe, became immensely popular with the preschool set, and a vodka-laced version appealed to the young party crowd. Even president-elect Bill Clinton dined on Bing Cherry Jell-O Salad for his first post-election Thanksgiving and Christmas.

Not bad for something made of artificial flavor, artificial color, fresh and frozen pork skins, cattle bones and hides, and assorted connective tissue from both animals.

Other Jell-O facts:

• Three out of four American houses have at least one package of Jell-O in the pantry.

• America eats an average of eight boxes of Jell-O every second of the day.

• The Jell-O capital of America is Grand Rapids, Michigan, which consumes 82 percent more Jell-O per capita than average. Why? Maybe because of all the Protestant churches. Another strange, hopefully unrelated, fact: Grand Rapids is also the largest per capita buyer of rat poison.

• The most popular flavor? Red (strawberry, raspberry and cherry). Jell-O has grown from four flavors in 1897 (orange, lemon, strawberry, and raspberry) to twenty today, including recent additions blueberry and watermelon.

• The key to hosting the ever-popular spectator sport called Jell-O Wrestling? Use an 8-foot square padded box, pour in 55 gallons of powder, add boiling water, chill for two days, and don't allow contestants to hold their opponents' heads under the Jell-O.

How Bic Got Its Ball Rolling

Look carefully at the point of a ballpoint pen. There's a tiny little ball there, of course, which transports the ink from the ink reservoir onto the paper. It looks simple, and in theory it is. But actually developing a usable ballpoint pen wasn't as easy as it looks. If it were, the pen in your pocket would be a Loud instead of a Bic, Parker, or Scripto.

John J. Loud of Massachusetts patented a "rolling-pointed fountain marker" on October 30, 1888. It used a tiny, rotating ball bearing that was constantly bathed on one side in ink. Over the next thirty years, 350 similar ballpoint patents were issued by the U.S. Patent Office. But none of the products appeared on the market. The main problem was getting the ink right. If it was too thin, the pens blotched on paper and leaked in pockets. If it was too thick, the pens clogged. Under controlled circumstances, it was sometimes possible to mix up a batch ink that did what it was supposed to do . . . at least until the temperature changed. The best they could do was a ballpoint that would (usually) work fine at 70° F., but would clog at temperatures below 64° and leak, blotch and smear at temperatures above 77°.

At least that's how it was until the Biro brothers decided to take the challenge on. After World War I, eighteen-year-old Ladislas Biro, newly discharged from the Hungarian army, tried out a number of career options. He studied medicine, art, and hypnotism, but none of the fields held his interest long enough to become a career. Eventually, he fell into newspaper work.

In 1935, Biro was editing a small newspaper and found

himself cursing his fountain pen. The ink soaked into paper's newsprint like a sponge, allowing the pen's sharp tip to shred it into soggy pulp. Even when he was working with a decent quality of paper, the ink left smudges on his fingers and clothes—and had to be refilled too often. He recruited his brother Georg, a chemist. The brothers Biro started designing new pens.

After trying dozens of new pen designs and ink formulations, Ladislas and Georg, unaware that it had already been done at least 351 times before, invented the ballpoint pen.

Vacationing together at a resort on the shores of the Mediterranean, the two brothers began talking to an older gentleman about their new invention. They showed him a working model, and he was suitably impressed. It just so happened that the elderly gentleman was the president of Argentina, Augustine Justo, who suggested that the brothers open a pen factory in his country.

A few years later, World War II began, and the Biros fled Hungary. They remembered their old pal, the president of Argentina, and set sail for South America. They landed in Buenos Aires with ten dollars between them. Justo remembered them and, with his help, they lined up several investors. By 1943 they had set up their manufacturing plant.

The results were spectacular. A spectacular failure, that is. They had made the mistake that all of their forerunners had made—they depended on gravity to move the ink onto the ball. That meant that the pens had to be held straight up and down at all times. Even then, the ink flow was irregular, leaving heavy globs.

Ladislas and Georg returned to the lab and came up with a new design. This one depended on capillary action instead of gravity, siphoning the ink toward the point no matter what position the pen was held in. Within a year, the Biros had brought out their new improved model in Argentina, but the pens didn't sell very well. The Biros ran out of money and stopped production.

However, the U.S. Air Force came to the rescue. American flyers, sent to Argentina during the war, discovered that the ballpoints worked upside down and at high altitudes without having to be refilled very often. The wartime U.S. Department of State attempted to get American manufacturers to manufacture a similar pen. The Eberhard Faber Company, in an attempt to corner the market, paid $500,000 for the U.S. rights to the ballpoint, yielding the Biro brothers their first profitable year ever.

About this time a Chicagoan named Milton Reynolds ran across the Biro pen in Argentina. He came back to the United States and discovered that similar pens had been patented by John J. Loud and other Americans, but that the patents had expired. He therefore figured he could get away with copying the Biro design. He sold his ballpoint pens for $12.50 through Gimbels department store in New York City. They were such a novelty that Gimbels sold out its entire stock on the first day—a total of ten thousand pens.

Various manufacturers jumped on the bandwagon. Reynolds hired swimming star Esther Williams to show that the pen would write underwater; other manufacturers showed their pens writing upside down or through stacks of a dozen pieces of carbon paper.

There was a problem, though: Despite the hoopla, ballpoint pens still didn't work very dependably. They leaked, ruining many a document and good shirt. They plugged up. Sales started going down, as did prices. The pens, once an expensive luxury, began selling for as little as nineteen cents. But even at that price, people bought one, tried it, and—frustrated—vowed never to buy another ballpoint as long as they lived.

The man to eventually change their mind was Marcel Bich from France. As a manufacturer of penholders and cases, he watched with professional interest as the ballpoint industry first took off and then began crashing to the ground. He was interested in the innovative design of the ballpoint pen, but was appalled at the high cost and low quality. He determined that he could take over much of the ballpoint market if he could come up with a dependable pen at a low cost.

The Biro brothers licensed their patents to Bich, who went to work. For two years, he bought samples of every ballpoint pen on the market and systematically tested them, looking for their strengths and weaknesses. In 1952, Bich unveiled his triumph: a six-sided, inexpensive, clear plastic ballpoint pen that wrote smoothly and didn't leak or jam. Looking at the international market, he figured that his name would be a problem in America. Rather than risk having his product referred to as a "bitch pen," he modified the spelling of his name so it would be pronounced correctly everywhere his pen was sold—Bic.

The basic Bic ballpoint was an immediate hit all over the world. Billions of them, their style essentially unchanged in the years since, have been sold, used, misplaced, disassembled, lost, and disposed of. While Bic has expanded into other pen designs and even diversified into other products, the basic cheap but dependable Bic pen continues to be responsible for a large chunk of the company's yearly profits.

Why Coke Hates Pepsi (and Vice Versa)

In business, there is often competition, healthy and otherwise. There are even bitter rivalries and grudges. But few competitors have gone after each other with the battle-scarred, no-holds-barred, take-no-prisoners fervor of Coke and Pepsi. This is a grudge match, a Hatfield and McCoy feud that goes back several generations.

How and when did it start? It depends on who you ask. But to understand it, you have to go back to the beginning.

It was May 1886, in Atlanta. Still smarting and depressed by its defeat in the Civil War, the South turned en masse for solace to fundamentalist religion and patent medicines. The cure-all "snake oils" of the North tended to be heavy on alcohol, but Southerners were immersed in a period of Bible-thumpin' anti–demon rum sentiments. Patent medicine makers in the South began replacing alcohol with another active ingredient that was believed to be safe, healthy, and morally pure. That ingredient was cocaine.

Atlanta druggist John Styth Pemberton, under pressure from local Temperance activists, had for the last six months been reformulating his "French Wine Coca—Ideal Brain Tonic" to remove the alcohol and replace it with another ingredient that would give the same kick.

He found it in the kola nut, a stimulant that slaves had brought with them from Africa that had the reputation of being a wonder hangover cure. He blended it with the coca extract, for the first time bringing together the two strongest stimulants known at the time, and found that the concoction was indeed a potent "brain tonic." Unfortunately, it tasted terrible. So the gray-bearded druggist spent months hunched over a thirty-gallon brass kettle in his backyard mixing up dozens of concoctions, before finally settling on what he decided was the ideal mixture of oils, herbs, and extracts to mask the flavor of the potently psychoactive mix.

Coca-Cola was not yet visualized as a carbonated drink. It was a thick, sweet brown syrup, packaged in reused beer bottles, that Pemberton sold to other Atlanta drugstores for twenty-five cents a bottle. The druggists would sell the entire bottle or administer individual doses of the "Intellectual Beverage and Temperance Drink," often mixed into a glass of tap water to make it a little easier to get down. It became moderately successful as pick-me-up and as a hangover remedy for those Southerners who hadn't yet succumbed to the antibooze hysteria around them.

That summer an earthshaking event happened in Jacob's Drug Store, one of Coca-Cola's outlets in Atlanta. A customer came in complaining of a severe hangover. Handed a bottle of Coca-Cola syrup, he asked Willis E. Venable, the soda fountain man, to open it and mix it with water right there so he could get immediate relief. Rather than walk to the water tap at the back of the store, Venable asked if the man minded soda water. The distressed customer wasn't particular. He gulped the fizzing mixture and said, "Say, this is really fine. Much better than using plain water like the label says." Word got around, and people started requesting the bubbly version all over town.

Pemberton was taken aback. He had been marketing Coca-Cola as a medicine "for all nervous afflictions—Sick Headache, Neuralgia, Hysteria, Melancholia, Etc." He hadn't even considered that it might be drunk for recreation. Nevertheless, he saw the opportunity and jumped, modifying mixing instructions on the syrup's labels and changing his ads to note that "Coca-Cola makes a delicious, exhilarating, refreshing, and invigorating beverage" in addition to its medicinal qualities.

That same summer, Atlanta passed its first dry laws, making alcohol illegal. Coke syrup sales jumped from twenty-five gallons that year to 1,049 gallons the next, largely through the marketing efforts of Pemberton's associate and financial backer Frank M. Robinson, who coined the name of the drink, created Coke's first ads and promotions, and drew the ornate-script "Coca-Cola" logo that is still used today. Robinson was a shrewd salesman and promoter. He had met Pemberton when trying to sell him some real estate; Pemberton, instead, sold Robinson on the potential of his new Ideal Brain Tonic. Robinson came to work on Coca-Cola and stayed on through several changes of ownership until his retirement nearly thirty years later.

In 1887, despite consuming large quantities of his health tonic, Pemberton's health began to fail. Furthermore, Coke sales were still not brisk enough to make him financially solvent. For a very modest amount of money, he sold two-thirds of his interest in the business to Willis Venable, the man who first brought the fizz to Coke. Pemberton's inventory, which he drew up at the time of the transfer, gives a clue to Coca-Cola's closely guarded secret ingredients: oil of lemon, oil of lime, oil of nutmeg, fluid extract of nutmeg, fluid extract of coca leaves, vanilla, citric acid, orange elixir, oil of neroli, and caffeine.

Pemberton died destitute on August 16, 1888, and was buried in an unmarked pauper's grave. (It wasn't until seventy years later that the founder of the Coca-Cola company was finally provided a headstone.) Before he died, he sold the last of his stock to Asa Candler, a more prosperous fellow druggist. With the help of two partners, Candler quietly bought up all the rest of the stock in Coca-Cola from Venable and other investors. Full ownership of the company—lock, stock, and secret formula—cost Candler a grand total of $2,300.

Candler was a devout Christian and teetotaler, and he wholeheartedly believed that Coke was the ideal temperance drink and all-purpose medicine. Ironically, in light of the New Coke uproar a hundred years later, he and Frank Robinson immediately set to work reformulating Pemberton's original recipe to improve the taste and shelf life while keeping the same heart-pounding jolt of coca leaves, kola nuts, and caffeine.

Candler reformulated Coke again a few years later when anticocaine hysteria hit a peak. Newspapers carried shameless, race-baiting stories about crazed "negroes" rampaging with insatiable lust, superhuman strength, and even enhanced marksmanship as a result of cocaine. Slang terms for an order of Coca-Cola quickly expanded from "a Coke" to "a cold dope" and "a shot in the arm"; soda fountains became "hop joints" and "dope stores." In 1903, Coca-Cola quietly switched to a new recipe that used coca leaves that had already been decocainized. (Coca-Cola continues to use spent coca leaves. It obtains them from the Stepan Chemical Company in New Jersey, the only legal processor of medical cocaine in the United States.)

A soldier named Benjamin Franklin Thomas, stationed in Cuba during the Spanish-American War, saw the Cubans drinking something called Pina Fria from bottles. Suffering from Coke withdrawal, he wondered: Why not bottle it pre-mixed in fizzy water and make it available everywhere? When Thomas got back to the United States, he and a partner named Joseph Whitehead called on Candler who, seeing little profit in the venture, signed over bottling rights to them.

Company legend has it that Candler had earlier paid a large sum to an acquaintance who came to his office claiming that he had the secret for vastly expanding Coca-Cola profits. Upon receiving the check, the man leaned over and whispered into Candler's ear: "Bottle it." According to the story, Candler didn't follow the advice because the bottles made back then tended to explode now and again, resulting in lawsuits. Whether the story is true or not, Candler made sure that Thomas and his partner signed an agreement holding him legally blameless if any of their bottles exploded.

Thomas and Whitehead, however, didn't have enough capital on hand to open even one bottling plant. Instead, they began selling regional bottling franchises.

Candler, in a mixture of Southern Methodist piety and good business sense, began lobbying aggressively for antialcohol laws all over the South. By 1907, 825 of the 994 counties in the former Confederacy had gone dry. National Prohibition came along thirteen years later. Through it all, sales of Coca-Cola soared.

Its success spawned dozens of imitators. In 1916 alone, busy Coke attorneys went after 153 wannabes with names like Cafe Cola, Afri-Cola, Charcola, Co-Co-Colian, Dope, Kola Kola, Pau-Pau Cola, King Kola, Fig Cola, Sola Cola, Candy Cola, Toca-Cola, Cold Cola, Kos Kola, Cay-Ola, Coke Ola, Koca-Nola, Kel Kola, Kaw-Kola, Co Kola, Kola-Nola, Caro-Cola, and Coca-Kola. By 1926, Coke attorney Harold Hirsch had run more than seven thousand competitors out of business, suing anybody with a similar name or script logo, and averaging a lawsuit a week. He even went after colors that he thought were distinctively Coke-related: Any soft drink company that sold its syrups in red barrels, for instance, or that had a syrup that was a dark caramel brown color.

The company began searching for a unique bottle design—one, as Thomas put it, "which a person will recognize as a Coca-Cola bottle even when he feels it in the dark. The bottle should be so shaped that, even when broken, a person could tell at a glance what it was."

After a succession of rejected designs, the bottlers adopted the now-classic bottle designed by the C.J. Root Company of Terre Haute, Indiana. The alternately tapered and bulging shape was brilliant artistry, but lousy botany: The designers thought they were copying the shape of the coca bean, but in fact they copied the *cocoa* bean, from which chocolate is made.

This hobbleskirt bottle (named after a short-lived fashion from 1914) was a huge success. Industrial designer Raymond Loewy called it a "perfectly formed" design, an "aggressively female" subliminal form that pleases men and women alike. Bottlers liked it because its extra-thick glass gave a heft that disguised how little Coca-Cola was actually in it (6½ ounces). And, best of all, it gave the company one more weapon against infringers.

PEPSI COMES ALIVE

But despite the new bottles and Hirsch's constant lawsuits, one Coke-wannabe prevailed and thrived.

Like Coke, Pepsi-Cola came from the South and was formulated by a former Confederate Army officer. Caleb B. Brabham had been forced to quit medical school when his father's business failed. In 1893, he started a pharmacy in New Bern, North Carolina, which thrived because it provided a soda fountain alternative to the discredited saloons of the town. Like other druggists, Brabham began tinkering with new elixirs and patent medicines, using the knowledge he had picked up in medical school.

He modeled a concoction after Coca-Cola, which was becoming wildly popular. Intended to relieve stomach disorders and ulcers, "Brad's Drink," as it was called, was a pleasant mixture of vanilla, exotic oils and spices, sugar, and the African kola nut. It became popular with the locals. He renamed it Pepsi-Cola and in 1902 started peddling it to other soda fountains. In 1904, he sold shares in the business and copied Coke's franchise system to begin marketing Pepsi in bottles. By 1909, Brabham had 250 bottlers in twenty-four states. He was getting rich.

World War I changed all that. Rapidly fluctuating sugar prices and labor costs crippled the company. By 1922, the Pepsi Company was bankrupt and Brabham went back to filling prescriptions at his New Bern drug store.

A Wall Street money man named Roy C. Megargel bought up the company's trademark and assets and started up a new Pepsi-Cola Company in Richmond, Virginia. But he faltered at coming up with enough investment capital to keep it going. The Pepsi-Cola Company went down in flames again in 1932.

Next came Charles Guth, president of Loft, Inc., a candy company in Long Island. Guth had a grudge against the Coca-Cola Company for not giving him a volume discount on the 31,000 gallons of Coke syrup he bought each year for his 115 soda fountains. He decided to make his own beverage, so he took $10,500 out of Loft's till to buy up the Pepsi rights, including Megargel as a silent partner, and started still another new Pepsi-Cola Company in Long Island. He tinkered with the recipe according to his own taste preferences ("New Pepsi!") and began serving Pepsis in his stores.

Coca-Cola sent its undercover agents into Loft stores and filed a lawsuit, claiming that they had fraudulently been served Pepsi-Cola when they had ordered Coca-Cola. Guth countersued, claiming that Coke was illegally harassing and maligning his stores and employees. The bitter court case would be played out in slow motion over the following decade.

Meanwhile, however, the Pepsi-Cola Company had other troubles. With Loft stores as its only outlet, the company was losing money fast, and Guth decided he wanted out. He even offered to sell Pepsi to the archenemy, Coca-Cola, for a modest price. In the blunder of its life, Coke turned him down. Meanwhile, his partner, Megargel, sued for funds Guth owed him, so Guth bought him out for $35,000, of which all but $500 came out of Loft's company funds.

Pepsi, now 91 percent owned by Guth, was about to go under for a third time, when a used bottle dealer convinced Guth to start bottling his drink in used beer bottles. Since they held nearly twice as much as Coke's 6½-ounce bottle, he decided to charge twice as much as well. But the Depression was on, and ten cents was more than people were willing to pay for a soda.

Guth dropped his price to a nickel and advertised that Pepsi was offering twice as much for the same price as a Coke. Pepsi's sales went through the roof. However, while Guth sold soft drinks, his candy stores were falling apart. Stockholders revolted, and he resigned his presidency.

The new president ordered an audit and found that Guth had financed Pepsi with Loft funds. The company sued Guth. After a bruising battle, the court ruled that Loft, Inc., was the legitimate owner of Pepsi-Cola. In spring of 1939, Guth was handed $300,000 and shown the door. Loft, Inc., took possession of his thriving multinational, multimillion-dollar company.

Coke noted Pepsi's growth with alarm. The battle escalated beyond sending undercover agents into Loft stores: In 1938, Coke sued Pepsi over trademark violations, claiming proprietary rights over the name "Cola." On the first day of the trial, Coke lawyers made a big show of hauling out huge stacks of legal documents detailing its victories over other trademark infringers.

From the weighty precedence, it looked like an open and

shut case. The widow of the victim of an earlier Coke lawsuit called on Walter Mack, the new president of Pepsi, to offer condolences. Her husband had been president of something called Cleo Cola. In passing, she mentioned that the Coca-Cola Company had given her husband a $35,000 check to put him out of business.

A payoff? Mack couldn't believe his ears. So maybe Coke wasn't so sure of victory after all. The next day Pepsi lawyers asked about the check, and Coke's lawyers asked for a two-day recess to respond. That afternoon, Coke president Robert Woodruff called Mack and invited him to meet the next morning. According to Mack the conversation went like this:

"Mr. Mack, I've been thinking about this lawsuit, and I think we ought to settle it. Is that agreeable to you?"

"It is, under one condition."

Mack took a piece of paper and wrote, "I, Robert Woodruff, president and chief executive officer of the Coca-Cola Company, hereby agree that the corporation will recognize the Pepsi-Cola trademark and never attack it in the United States." He handed it to Woodruff. Woodruff drafted a similar agreement stating that Pepsi would recognize Coke. Both men signed.

The truce didn't last long. Coke, noting the agreement applied only to the United States, dispatched attorneys to file trademark violation suits in countries all over the world. A judge in Canada first ruled for Coke, but Canada's Supreme Court ruled for Pepsi. Because it was a member of the British Commonwealth, Coke appealed to the highest Commonwealth court, the Privy Council in England.

"It was a hell of a dirty trick," observed Mack later, "because is was during the war and they had lawyers over there. The Privy Council had set a date, and Coke figured we wouldn't be able to get anybody over there." Pepsi hired Wendell Willkie, who had just finished his unsuccessful presidential bid. Willkie was able to get the government to fly him over to England in an Air Force bomber, ostensibly to make speeches for the war effort, and he got there in time to represent Pepsi in the courts. The Privy Council ruled in favor of Pepsi's claim that "cola" was a generic term and requested that both companies coexist in peace.

But that wasn't going to happen. Although the suits and countersuits stopped, the two companies continued to slash at each other in the marketplace and through their extraordinary governmental connections (Pepsi generally has connections among the Republicans; Coke, among the Democrats). Coke got itself adopted as a quasigovernment agency in World War II to boost the morale and energy levels of fighting boys and munitions workers, spreading its market worldwide at government expense. Coke was named a "war priority item," shipped in the same boats as food and ammunition. After the war, fifty-nine new Coke plants were installed at U.S. government expense to help rebuild Europe. (Ironically, considering Coke's wartime posture as all-American, Coca-Cola continued bottling in Nazi Germany through the war, with the syrup smuggled in through contacts in the international business community and the Nazi government.)

One of Coke's officers served as a consultant to the Beverage and Tobacco board, which (according to Pepsi president Mack) he used to help Coke and hinder Pepsi. For example, one of his first directives limited sugar users to 80 percent of their 1941 consumption. That was acceptable for Coke's long-successful bottling operation, but many of Pepsi's bottlers were not even established in 1941. After the war, Pepsi accused Coke of working to extend sugar rationing beyond necessity. While Coke extended its influence deeper into the Democratic executive branch, Pepsi courted Republicans, most notably

Senator Joe McCarthy who, in exchange for a $20,000 loan, became known in the Senate as the Pepsi-Cola Kid. Two decades later, Pepsi would hire defeated presidential candidate Richard Nixon as their chief counsel. (Conspiracy buffs take note: Nixon was in Dallas on November 22, 1963, attending a Pepsi convention.) Pepsi later helped bankroll Nixon's successful presidential bid.

Pepsi and Coke fought it out in the advertising world as well, trading slogans and marketing punches left and right. Both used elaborate advertising campaigns and giveaways. Pepsi, for example, bought the exclusive rights to the new skywriting process in the 1930s and wrote PEPSI-COLA over nearly every city in America. Coke's ads usually centered on cementing its image as an all-American institution; Pepsi's on being the upstart challenger favored by youth and other nonstodgy types. It even changed its formula one more time in 1950 to make Pepsi more appealing to that market.

The Cola Wars continue.

How Silly Putty Bounced Back from Oblivion

Something funny happened when the government began seeking an inexpensive rubber substitute during World War II. At General Electric's New Haven laboratory, chemical engineer James Wright was working on that problem. He mixed silicone oil and boric acid in a test tube. They combined into a gooey pink polymer. Excited, he tossed some down on the counter.

Boing! To his surprise, it bounced right back at him.

With high hopes, GE sent glops of the substance to scientists around the world, challenging them to find practical uses for it. They couldn't come up with any. Not that they didn't try. One scientist, noting that it retained its strange properties down to −70° F., tested it to see if it would work as an insulating or caulking material in Arctic climes. No such luck.

"Bouncing putty," as GE dubbed it, languished in limbo. Still, fun-loving GE scientists started mixing up small batches for parties. At one such affair in Connecticut in 1949, a chunk was passed to Peter Hodgson, Sr., high school dropout, advertising consultant, and bon vivant. As he fingered and massaged the chunk, the phrase "silly putty" suddenly came to him. Although already $12,000 in debt, he borrowed $147 more and bought twenty-one pounds of the putty from GE at seven dollars a pound. He packed it into little plastic eggs and began selling it as an adult toy at an incredible markup (two dollars per half-ounce).

Hodgson was doing pretty well, selling as many as three hundred eggs a day at a few outlets, when the *New Yorker* featured the putty in a small story. Within days, he received orders for 230,000 eggs. Silly Putty, "the toy with one moving part," was on its way to becoming a national mania.

Originally, adults were the target market. Hodgson believed that kids wouldn't appreciate the putty's richness and subtlety: "It appeals to people of superior intellect," he told a reporter. "The inherent ridiculousness of the material acts as an emotional release to hard-pressed adults."

That marketing strategy worked at first, but after about five years the market changed from "80 percent adults to 20 percent children" to a ratio of 20 percent adults to 80 percent children.

Kids loved the stuff—so much so that the manufacturer had to go back to the labs to reformulate it. The problem was a stack of complaints from parents about Silly Putty getting permanently into hair, clothing, upholstery, and carpeting. The Silly Putty of today is less sticky than that made forty years ago, and the company now has a toll-free line that offers advice on how to get Silly Putty unstuck from things.

And the world has finally discovered practical uses for Silly Putty. It has been used by astronauts to hold tools in place while in zero-gravity, in physical therapy clinics to reduce stress and strengthen hands and wrists, and at the Cincinnati Zoo to make casts of the hands and feet of its gorillas.

Corporate Culture

Grow industry, grow, grow, grow! Harmony and sincerity! Matsushita Electric!
— Matsushita Electric Company's company song,
sung by its employees every morning

Women on certain jobs are every bit as good as men. For instance, we wouldn't think of having a man sell brassieres.
— Drummond Bell,
Montgomery Ward vice president

The average man won't really do a day's work unless he is caught and cannot get out of it. There is plenty of work to do, if people would do it.
— Henry Ford, during the Great Depression

This is rat eat rat, dog eat dog. I'll kill 'em, and I'm going to kill 'em before they kill me. You're talking about the American way of survival of the fittest.
— Ray Kroc

THE AXE FALLS

One suddenly out-of-favor executive at Ford Motor Company learned that he had been fired when he came in one morning and found that someone had hacked his desk to pieces with an axe.

How We Got Stuck on Those Little Yellow Post-it Things

Do you remember life without Post-it Notes? Can you *imagine* life without them? A lot of people in offices, publishing houses, art studios, and medical practices simply cannot. They seem like such a logical and obvious product—something that can be stuck to anything and yet taken off cleanly, allowing corrections, comments, and notices without leaving a trace. Yet, Post-its failed dismally in its first four test markets and almost didn't make it to market.

The Minnesota Mining and Manufacturing Company (3-M) began in 1902 as a comedy of errors. Even the set-up sounds like the beginning of a joke: There were these five Minnesotans, see?—a doctor, a lawyer, two railroad executives, and the manager of a meat market.

The five investors didn't know much about sandpaper, but they knew the mineral corundum was in heavy demand as the "sand." They were given the splendid opportunity to buy a corundum mine on the shores of Lake Superior near Duluth. In retrospect, they probably should have added a sixth partner, preferably a mineralogist, because after the five had taken on other investors, hired workers, invested in machinery, and begun a full-scale mine, they discovered that they had bought a conundrum instead of corundum. They sent samples from their mine to a sandpaper manufacturer and found that the granules were "fool's corundum"—completely unusable for manufacturing sandpaper or much of anything else.

What were they going to do? Still fixated, for some reason, on making it big in sandpaper, the investors decided to buy corundum from somewhere else and become manufacturers instead of miners. Fittingly, competition in the sandpaper business was rough, even abrasive, and the new company got clobbered in the marketplace. Forced to innovate or die, it developed an abrasive cloth for polishing metal. Then, a staff inventor named Francis G. Okie came up with Wetordry, a waterproof, reduced-dust sandpaper made from aluminum oxide, which was adopted by the auto industry.

He also came up with the bright idea of marketing sandpaper as a safe substitute for shaving with a razor blade. Even though Okie sanded his chin smooth for the rest of his life, the idea didn't catch on with the rest of the shaving public. The important thing is this 3-M tradition of trying to find radical new uses for established materials: It led to Post-it Notes . . . eventually. But it was a long and dubious trip.

Every few years, 3-M puts together a polymers-for-adhesives team to review new materials that might look promising for, say, making the glue on their cellophane tape a little more permanent. Chemist Spencer Silver was named to the team when it convened in 1964. He started looking into a new family of monomers (the Tinkertoylike basic molecules that can be joined to make more elaborate polymers) developed by Archer Daniels Midland, Inc. While doing the systematic monkeying around that scientists call basic research, he added more than the recommended dose of the chemical reactant that hooks the monomers together into polymer chains.

"I wanted to see what would happen," Silver recalled. "If I had sat down and factored it out beforehand or cracked the research books, I probably wouldn't have done the experiment. The literature was full of examples that said you can't do this."

But he did. What he got was something totally unexpected. It was a liquid that was milky white until you put it under pressure. Then it turned crystal clear. That was interesting, but so what? He tried it as an adhesive. He characterized it as "tacky" but not "aggressively adhesive." Silver also found that it was narcissistic—it tended to get stuck on itself more than it wanted to stick to anything else. If you put it on one surface and stuck a piece of paper on it, either *all* of the adhesive or *none* of the adhesive would come off when you peeled off the paper. The adhesive stuck ambivalently to everything it touched.

Silver was intrigued with the stuff. The rest of the company was less so, trapped in a paradigm that the only good adhesive was one that stuck more or less permanently. Eventually, the company disbanded the polymers group and reassigned everybody to new responsibilities. But Silver continued playing with his polymer, emboldened by a 3-M dictum that encourages employees to spend 15 percent of their time on pet projects and hunches. (That system hasn't always worked without snags. One 3-M scientist spent 15 percent of his time seeking a use for the company's ample stock of false corundum. But his 15 soon became 20 percent, then more. He became obsessed with the project to the detriment of his other work, and the company fired him. The funny thing is, losing his job didn't stop him. He continued coming to work every morning as if nothing had happened, and the company eventually rehired him. He finally discovered that the sandy mineral could be used in roofing materials. Years later, he retired as a vice president.)

Traditionally, employees at 3-M can also take their pet projects to other departments if their own departments don't okay them. Silver couldn't get his immediate superiors excited, so he wandered the hallways of 3-M giving demonstrations and presentations, crying out like a demented prophet in a corporate wilderness, "But it must be good for something!" His coworkers were usually polite, but uncertain how to proceed after his now-it-sticks, now-it-doesn't presentations. He had to nearly beg the company to patent the new polymer. To humor Silver, an otherwise sterling employee, 3-M patented it, but—to save money—only in the United States, not internationally.

"You have to be a zealot at times in order to keep interest alive, because it will die off," remarked Silver. Somebody finally came up with a product using Silver's polymer: a no-pin sticky bulletin board. It died a lingering death. But Silver wouldn't quit, thinking there must be some better use for his polymer. "Sometimes I was so angry because this new thing was so obviously unique. I'd tell myself, 'Why can't you think of a product? It's your job!'"

In 1974, someone finally came up with a problem to match Silver's solution. He was Arthur Fry, 3-M chemist, amateur mechanic, and church choir director. He had seen one of Silver's demonstrations years before and had kept it in the back of his mind in case some idea came up.

Perhaps it was divine inspiration. One Sunday morning, as always, Fry had marked songs in his hymnal with little scraps of paper. While signaling to the choir to stand, he fumbled his hymnal and the scraps of paper fluttered to the floor like snow. While frantically finding his place, he thought, "Gee, a little adhesive on these bookmarks, that would be just the ticket." Suddenly he remembered Silver's now-it-sticks, now-it-doesn't demonstration, and he started thinking of situations where semisticky paper might be real helpful.

On Monday, he came to work early. He found there were still problems to work out, like how to make sure the adhesive didn't come off on the document. Company chemists came up with a substrate paper coating that made the adhesive stick firmly to the paper. There was another problem: 3-M's mechanical engineers said it was impossible to apply the adhesive to paper in a continuous roll, which made the product impractical to make. Fry designed a machine he thought would do the trick and assembled it in his basement at home. Unfortunately, it was bigger than his basement doorway, so he had to knock out part of his basement wall to transport it to work.

Fry and his team began producing prototype Post-its in the now-classic yellow color. As a form of informal marketing research, they began distributing them to offices around the building. "Once people started using them it was like marijuana," said a team member with a shaky grasp of pharmacology. "Once you start using it, you can't stop."

But despite in-house addiction, the 3-M marketing department didn't believe the little yellow sheets could be sold outside the company in any significant numbers. Even after they had become as hooked on the product as everybody else in the company, they kept asking the question: Why would anybody buy this "glorified scratch paper" for a dollar a package? Their lack of enthusiasm showed up in their promotional strategy in a four-city test market. They simply described the product, and didn't include samples. There was just no way for people to imagine the uses for the new product—they had to try it out for themselves. Not surprisingly, the Post-its failed the four-city test miserably.

Fry's boss, Geoff Nicholson, looking at the thousands of Post-its circulating around the company, couldn't believe that they wouldn't succeed if marketed properly. He recruited his boss, Joe Ramey, to go with him out in the field and see what was wrong. Ramey agreed to go along, not so much because he believed in the product, but mostly to humor Nicholson. They went to one of the four cities, Richmond, Virginia, to talk directly with people who might find Post-its useful.

This was yet another of those 3-M traditions. In its early

years, under the inspiration of William L. McKnight, 3-M's sales force would not make a pitch to a purchasing agent until they had talked their way onto the floor and demonstrated their products to the workers who would use them. This not only created a demand for the products, but sometimes inspired new ones because the sales reps were trained to look for new ways to use and improve their products. One rep who saw auto workers struggling with painting two-tone trim on cars came up with the idea of masking tape. (The company made it with two narrow strips of adhesive on the back, one running along each edge. An auto worker complained that 3-M should put adhesive all over the back of the tape instead of just on its edges. "What's with this 'Scotch' tape?" he asked, referring to an ethnic stereotype of stinginess. The company adopted his suggestion, and then decided "Scotch" would make a pretty good name for the new product.)

Fry and Nicholson trudged around Richmond's business district, handing out packs of Post-its, sticking them on things, and showing what they were good for. From the enthusiastic response they got, it was clear that people would use them, show them to their friends and, yes, even buy them. They left Richmond at the end of the day with a fistful of orders. Based on this admittedly anecdotal data, the company decided to try again in a one-shot, for-the-marbles blitz of a test market. They rolled their heavy-gun sales reps into the town of Boise, Idaho.

The reps blanketed Boise's businesses with free samples and order forms. They got a 90 percent reorder response from the companies they gave samples to—more than twice the 40 percent rate that the company would consider a success.

Post-its went into full national distribution in 1980 with direct-mail pieces and giveaway offers in business magazines. They caught on across America. Since then, they've become an international hit as well, sometimes with necessary adaptations. In Japan, for instance, they are long and narrow in shape to accommodate the vertical writing of Japanese characters.

"The Post-it was a product that met an unperceived need," says Fry. "If you had asked somebody what they needed, they might have said a better paper clip. But give them a Post-it Note, and they immediately know what to do with it and see its value."

Gatorade Sweats It Out in the Market

Is drinking Gatorade while exercising any more effective than water? Several studies have suggested that the answer is no, unless you're involved in an extraordinary level of exertion, like running an ultramarathon. Regardless, Gatorade and the research that spawned it has done one undeniable service for the sports community: It broke down the dangerously misguided prohibition by old-style high school and college coaches against drinking liquids while exercising.

An idle question from a coach brought James Robert Cade, a kidney researcher at the University of Florida, into sports research in 1965. How come, asked Gator assistant coach DeWayne Douglas, football players never have to pee during games? Since they lose as much as fifteen pounds during a game, where does all that weight go? And why do his players seem to "run out of gas" during the fourth quarter?

Cade did some research and found that players playing hard in the Florida sun sweated at an amazing rate, losing, not just water, but also sodium and potassium. As a result, the players' kidneys shut down to conserve liquid.

Cade analyzed sweat and came up with a liquid of similar composition. He added a lime flavoring to make it more palatable, but kept the flavor as light as possible, figuring it would inspire players to drink more of it. He mixed up a huge quantity of the stuff and presented it to the coach.

When the University of Florida Gators started drinking it, they discovered that they didn't sag midway during the game—and that the heat didn't leave them as exhausted as before.

They even got used to the taste after a while. One player had complained that the concoction "tastes like pee." Cade, ever the scientist, went back to his lab, took a sample of his own urine, chilled it . . . and reported back to the player that "urine doesn't taste a bit like Gatorade."

The big jug of Gatorade on the sidelines developed a mystique among the Gators and eventually among the teams they played. In 1967, when Florida beat Georgia Tech 27–12 in the Orange Bowl, Tech's coach claimed they lost because "we didn't have Gatorade."

That year, Cade licensed the rights to Stokely–Van Camp, which began paying him a royalty on every drink sold. Jugs of Gatorade began appearing on the sidelines at professional football games, and coaches all over the country began changing a deeply held but completely erroneous belief. For decades, most had denied their athletes liquid during games and practices, thinking it would cause debilitating muscle cramps and worse. Athletes were allowed only damp towels to suck on when they got thirsty. As a result, about fifty student athletes died every year from heat stroke. Cade's research—and that highly visible jug on the sidelines of pro football games—convinced most coaches to change their ways. Today, heat stroke deaths have dropped to nearly zero.

When royalty money began pouring in, the University of Florida sued Cade, saying that it should own the rights to Gatorade because he was an employee at the time of his development. Cade countered that he had worked on Gatorade on his own time. In fact, early in the process, he had asked his department at the university to help him develop and patent the liquid, which would have given the University of Florida full rights to the drink. The department had turned him down.

The final court settlement gave Cade and his research team 80 percent of the profits and the rest—about $2 million a year—to the university.

How Cracker Jacks Became a Prized Snack Food

Jack Norworth and Albert von Tilzer wrote *Take Me Out to the Ballgame* in 1908, years before either one of them had actually seen a baseball game. They had both, however, eaten Cracker Jacks, so they included the famous line: "Buy me some peanuts and Cracker Jack, I don't care if I never come back . . ."

Like the Ferris wheel, the ice cream cone, and Aunt Jemima pancakes, Cracker Jacks appeared for the first time during the Columbia Exhibition in Chicago in 1893. In a sense, the popcorn snack had its roots in the Great Chicago Fire twenty-two years earlier. Frederick Rueckheim, a recent immigrant from Germany, was working on a farm in rural Illinois in 1871 when he heard that there were good-paying jobs in the city cleaning up the charred ruins and debris. Rueckheim stashed his life's savings of $200 in his pocket and went.

Once Rueckheim got there, the jobs weren't quite as good as promised, so he opened a one-popper popcorn stand with a partner, William Brinkmeyer. Their sales were brisk enough that they expanded to more and bigger stands—and finally to popcorn wholesaling. The burgeoning company outgrew its facilities six times in the next seven years. To help out, Frederick brought his brother, Louis, over from Germany. Louis soon bought out Brinkmeyer's half of the company, but Frederick made sure Louis knew whose half was the bigger half: He named the business F. W. Rueckheim & Brother.

In 1884, their factory burned down. The brothers quickly rebuilt, and within six months their business was popping again. They started expanding the popcorn line, adding marshmallows and other sweet flavorings to batches. For the Columbia Exhibition, the world's first World's Fair, they decided to mix up something new and different. The molasses, peanut, and popcorn mixture was a huge success, garnering orders from retailers all over the country. After yet another factory expansion, Frederick complained all the way to the bank: "No matter how we try to plan for it, the orders always exceed our production."

The still-unnamed product was shipped to retailers in large wooden tubs, but there was a problem. Due to heat and agitation, the popcorn often stuck together in one huge sticky glop. Louis went to work on the problem, and in 1896 discovered a process that kept the individual particles separate (the formula is still used by the company today and is guarded as a valuable trade secret).

But that's not all that happened in 1896. The sticky snack finally got a name. A sales rep was munching on some and he exclaimed, using Victorian slang for something very good, "That's a cracker jack!" Frederick ran down and trademarked the phrase. The rest is history. (It is sobering to realize that, had the product been born in a later decade, the caramelized corn might have been called "The Cat's Pajamas" or "Cool Stuff" or "One Groovy Thing, Man" or even "Awesome, Dude.")

Now that it had a name, Cracker Jacks needed a package and a gimmick. The package came from one Henry Eckstein in 1899. He developed a wax-sealed, moisture-proof, individual serving–sized box. It was this box that made the product portable enough that it could be sold anywhere snacks could be found, including baseball games—eventually spawning the aforementioned musical tribute.

The gimmick came because the product needed to differentiate itself from the hundreds of "carameled popcorns" that had sprung up with names like Yellow Kid, Honey Corn, Unoit, Goldenrod, Honey Boy, Kor-Nuts, Nutty Corn, Five Jacks, Maple Jack, and Sammy Jack. The brothers' first try was a coupon that could be saved and exchanged for merchandise, a system that had recently been pioneered by Sears and Roebuck. The Rueckheims printed the coupons and issued an illustrated catalog offering over three hundred household items, sporting accessories, and toys. Cracker Jacks sales picked up briefly, but leveled off again shortly afterward.

It was reportedly Louis who first suggested putting small toys *inside* the packages, figuring that kids were more likely to make repeat purchases if they received immediate gratification instead of having to save coupons. The combination of name recognition and the packaged premium spurred a national craze that resulted in peak sales in 1914.

Frederick later decided to add the sailor boy, Jack, and his dog, Bingo, to the package in a wartime salute to our fighting boys. (One sad footnote: The boy was modeled after Frederick's own beloved grandson Robert, who often wore a sailor suit. As the first of the new packages rolled off the presses, Robert got pneumonia and died. So, besides on Cracker Jacks packages, the logo can be seen on little Robert's tombstone in Chicago.)

Cracker Jacks toys at the time were of remarkable quality: little magnifying glasses, miniature books, metal whistles, strings of beads, baseball cards, spinning tops, metal trains and cars, and more. The high quality continued through two world wars and into the 1950s, when little plastic TVs and spaceships were premium items. Unfortunately, the prizes are nothing special in our time—the needs of high-speed packaging and a general stinginess by Borden, which bought the company in 1964, have reduced the prizes to little more than various little pieces of paper.

How Fighting the Kaiser Created Kleenex and Kotex

Most of the time new products are the result of seeing a perceived problem and trying to solve it. But sometimes innovations come as a result of having too much of something and trying to find a purpose for it. Kleenex and Kotex are an example of the latter.

Paper manufacturing went through a profound shift in the early part of this century. Up until that point, papermakers used the subjective skills of their workers to determine, for instance, if a batch of wood pulp was right. A master papermaker would stir, touch, sniff, sometimes even taste the pulp mixture—and make subtle adjustments to the mix before it went through the rollers. The results were surprisingly good.

But things began changing as the world became more mechanized. The new high-speed printing presses tolerated only certain standardized grades of paper, and papermakers were required to become more scientific in their approach. The scientists who took over from the old-style craftspeople began developing new products.

Kimberly-Clark had been making paper in Wisconsin since 1872. In 1914, they hired paper technician Ernst Mahler. A recent graduate from the Technical University of Darmstadt, Germany, Mahler had studied cellulose chemistry. He set up a laboratory across the street from Kimberly-Clark headquarters and convinced company president J. C. Kimberly to accompany him to Germany over the summer to check out some new products that had been developed over there, including a fluffy paper wadding product that absorbed liquids better than cotton.

While Mahler and Kimberly were in Germany, World War I broke out. They cut their trip short and hurried back to the United States with enough samples and formulae to begin developing their own version of the wadding material. Mahler tested a variety of native wood pulps before deciding that spruce trees yielded the longest and most absorbent fibers.

As the war got going full swing, a cotton shortage developed, giving Kimberly-Clark a ready market for their new product. Cellucotton, so called because it was like cotton but made from cellulose, was used as pads in bandages, filters in gas masks, and stuffing for emergency jackets. When America entered the war, Kimberly-Clark patriotically decided that they would sell Cellucotton to the War Department and the Red Cross at no profit.

When the war ended abruptly, Kimberly-Clark had partially filled orders for 750,000 pounds of Cellucotton from the government and Red Cross. Kimberly-Clark allowed them to cancel their orders without penalty, leaving the company with a huge unwanted surplus. Worse, the army had surplus Cellucotton too and began selling it to civilian hospitals for a ridiculously low price, killing the market for Kimberly-Clark's surplus. The company floundered around for new uses for the product until two good ones dropped into its lap.

KOTEX

One of Kimberly-Clark's wartime nonprofit customers had been the American Fund for the French Wounded. A grateful official of the organization knew that Kimberly-Clark's business had been hurt by canceled war orders and passed on some helpful information: During the war, French nurses had tried pads of Cellucotton during their periods and found that they made excellent disposable sanitary pads. Did Kimberly-Clark think that American women might be ready for a new product of this sort?

Up to that time, menstrual pads were made of felt and had to be washed after every use. Doing some extensive but very discreet market research, the company determined that women hated the felt pads and would very much welcome an alternative. Early in 1920, Kimberly-Clark began marketing the first disposable sanitary napkin under the name Cellunaps.

Marketing was a problem. Menstrual products were never displayed or advertised. Company marketers found that consumers were embarrassed to ask their pharmacists for the product because of the "naps" part of the name, short for napkins. They decided to change the name to one that was meaningless—that would not reveal anything in a crowded drugstore. They coined the word Kotex.

Even with the name change and an unrevealing package, to avoid embarrassing its customers, most stores would not display the merchandise. They kept it behind the counter. Many even demanded that the company take the extra step of wrapping the box in unprinted brown paper so that even the Kotex name would be hidden.

While Kimberly-Clark could see the need for discreet marketing, officials at the company refused to wrap the product. They were spending millions of dollars in advertising in women's magazines and felt that the product should be treated like any other consumer product. They encouraged retailers to take Kotex out from behind the counters and put it on display. It took a few years, but eventually retailers got with the program.

Meanwhile, letters to the company poured in, mostly favorable. Some women, however, asked questions that showed a deep ignorance of their bodies and the menstrual process. Kimberly-Clark beefed up its education division and began mailing out information packs, including a pamphlet about puberty called "Marjorie May's Twelfth Birthday," which met with a torrent of criticism from religious leaders, self-styled moralists, and others who believed that too much knowledge was a dangerous thing. Several states specifically banned "Marjorie May" and other similar mailings as being too sexually explicit. But women, unable to get the information elsewhere, continued ordering them and, eventually, the bans were lifted. Kimberly-Clark also worked with the Disney Company to create a color movie, "The Story of Menstruation" for schools, which has been seen by over seventy million boys and girls.

By 1939, use of the reusable felt pads was down to 20 percent. During World War II, large numbers of women entered the labor pool. Kimberly-Clark, in the spirit of patriotism and good marketing, made it a highest priority—despite war shortages—that war plants were well-equipped with Kotex feminine napkins. By 1947, use of old washable felt pads was down to below 1 percent.

KLEENEX

Meanwhile, Kimberly-Clark also decided to try manufacturing Cellucotton in thin sheets. Kleenex was the result. But they misjudged the market and almost had a flop.

Printed on the first boxes, each containing one hundred Cellucotton sheets, was "Kleenex Sanitary Cold Cream Remover." Kimberly-Clark thought that it had found a niche market as a disposable cloth for removing makeup and cold cream. It hadn't even occurred to them that the soft little sheets might have more universal uses as well.

One problem was the price: sixty-five cents per box. Knowing that sixty-five cents was more than common folk were likely to pay, they aimed for an upscale crowd, associating the Kleenex with wealth, glamour, and the theatrical crowd. They sent promotional samples to makeup artists in Hollywood and tried to capitalize on the fact that the best Hollywood stylists used the new "scientific way to remove cold cream." They even showed movie stars using the tissues after a long day of shooting. Despite the hype, the tissues achieved only lukewarm sales.

The Kimberly-Clark marketing people kept trying. They invented a way to make tissues pop up automatically by shuffling two piles of overlapping tissues together like a deck of cards. They introduced colors. The marketplace yawned, and sales stayed flat.

In 1930, a desperate marketing department decided to go and see why Kleenex was not playing in Peoria. They literally went to Peoria, Illinois, with clipboards and a series of questions, asking people if they had any suggestions, comments, ideas, hints—anything. They were surprised to find that nearly two-thirds of the people in Peoria who used Kleenex used them as disposable handkerchiefs, not as makeup removers.

The marketers headed back to the main office and immediately changed their advertising to reflect this newly discovered use. "Don't put a cold in your pocket!" said one ad. "During colds, smother sneezes with Kleenex tissues! Use once, then destroy, germs and all." The same ad also suggested using Kleenex tissues as a filter in the coffee maker. "Now my coffee's clearer—my husband's happier!" Within two years, sales increased fourfold. Kleenex—appropriately, considering all the tears and sniffling in the genre—became the sponsor of the first radio soap opera ever, "The Story of Mary Marlin."

Incidentally, Kleenex tissues were the reincarnation of a very old product. In the seventeenth century, the Japanese used "sneezing paper" (*hanagami*)—regular paper that they crumpled repeatedly to soften. In 1637, an English visitor wrote, "They blow their noses with a certain soft and tough kind of paper which they carry about them in small pieces, which having been used, they fling away as a filthy thing."

How Barney Became the Most Successful Extinct Being Ever (Except, of Course, Elvis)

How did a six foot, four inch purple and green dinosaur crawl out of Texas and capture the hearts and minds of two and three year olds everywhere?

First of all, there's the legend as told by the company and duly reported in *Time* and other news sources. Sheryl Leach, an ordinary mother and schoolteacher, was driving down the Central Expressway in Dallas in 1988 with her restless toddler, Patrick, wondering how she could keep him amused long enough to have a few minutes free to herself. At the time, Patrick would only sit still for one video, "Wee Sing," which featured brightly colored animated characters and upbeat music. Suddenly, the story goes, Leach had a vision, an inspiration, a flash of lightning. "The thought was, How hard could it be? I could do that," Leach told *Time*. So she recruited a schoolteacher friend, Kathy Parker, to help, borrowed some money, and voilà! A cottage industry of Barney tapes, sold by moms to moms in the manner of Mary Kay Cosmetics and Amway.

This story is a press agent's dream, too good to be true. The real story is not quite that simple.

Take that "Wee Sing" video. In one scene, a cuddly and lovable stuffed teddy bear comes to life and leads a group of children through a series of public domain songs in a moronic voice. Coincidentally, Barney was going to be a teddy bear, too, but the developers decided to get original—they changed him into a cuddly and lovable stuffed *dinosaur* that comes to life and leads a group of children through a series of public domain songs in a moronic voice.

Then there's that "simple schoolteacher" story. Actually, Leach was working as a software manager for a religious and educational publisher named DLM, Inc., which her father-in-law, Richard Leach, owned. Parker was an early childhood product manager for the same company. Perhaps not so coincidentally, DLM had just built video production facilities and was looking to branch into the lucrative childhood video market. Leach's daddy-in-law paid the $1 million necessary for developing the idea, and also pulled video education specialist Dennis DeShazer from a real estate training series and assigned him to the Barney project.

The first eight videos, costarring Sandy Duncan, sold more than four million copies. One of those copies came to the attention of Larry Rifkin, the executive vice president for programming at Connecticut Public Broadcasting.

It was Super Bowl Sunday. Rifkin took his four-year-old daughter to the video store to rent some tapes so he could watch the game in peace. "Leora walked out with 'Barney and the Backyard Gang' and she watched the program and watched the program and watched the program. So I decided to take a look and see what it was she was enjoying," said Rifkin. He tracked the manufacturer down and, not long after, contracted for the first thirty episodes, which have played over and over and over again on PBS. In 1992, PBS announced that it didn't have the money to shoot more episodes; besides, it didn't think that Barney was all that educational compared with their other programming for kids. An outpouring of calls and letters from long-suffering parents who had already involuntarily memorized all thirty episodes led PBS to announce they had scraped together $1.75 million to produce twenty new episodes which debuted in fall of 1993 and to ensure that Barney will be on PBS until at least 1998.

"The show was developed so that it's understandable for a two year old and can be enjoyed by a five-, six-, even seven-year-old child," Beth Ryan, communications and public relations manager for Barney, is quoted as saying, adding that unlike "Sesame Street" or "Rocky and Bullwinkle," there's not another level of meaning to entertain the poor adults who have to share a TV with the toddlers. "We're unique in that. We make a concentrated effort not to entertain adults." It works. Few adults are entertained, but in some time periods, 99 percent of all two to five year olds watching television are watching Barney.

Although company lawyers conducted searches to make sure that Barney's repertoire was completely in the public domain to avoid having to pay royalties to songwriters, they apparently slipped up. In a mom-and-kids exercise class, Parker heard a song to the tune of the public domain "This Old Man." The lawyers failed to find the owner of the words and an outraged songwriter/grandmother from Indiana stepped forward, saying that the Barney theme ("I love you / You love me / We're a happy family . . . ") was hers. DLM bought all rights to the song from her. They could afford to— they reportedly made $100 million from Barney merchandise in 1993 alone.

Say, maybe PBS should call Barney next time they have a pledge drive.

More Business Wisdom from the Sages

*Beware of the man who will not engage in idle conversation;
he is planning to steal your walking stick or water your stock.*
—William Emerson, 1906–1984

All business sagacity reduces itself in the last analysis to a judicious use of sabotage.
—Thorstein Veblen, 1857–1929

*Make three correct guesses consecutively and you will establish
a reputation as an expert.*
—Lawrence J. Peters

*There are the Trade-Unionists, once the oppressed, now the
tyrants, whose selfish and sectional pretensions need to be
bravely opposed.*
—John Maynard Keynes, 1883–1946

*People of the same trade seldom meet together, even for merriment and diversion, but the conversation ends in a conspiracy
against the public, or in some contrivance to raise prices.*
—Adam Smith, 1723–1790

Consumer Reports: Every Watchdog Has Its Day

Where do you turn before buying a car or major appliance? If you're like millions of folks, you go straight to the pages of the fiercely incorruptible *Consumer Reports*. *Reports* is published by the nonprofit, Yonkers-based Consumers Union, whose motto says it all: Test, Inform, Protect.

Consumer Reports has over 5 million subscribers today. Its subscription base zoomed up in the 1980s, partly because it was a time of conspicuous consumption. People needed advice before running up their Gold Mastercards. But consumers also figured they needed the protection from shoddy and unsafe products that government usually provides—but didn't during the Reagan Revolution.

Consumer Reports' impact goes far beyond its subscription numbers. If you go to a library, you'll find that its back issues are dog-eared and marked up for use. *Consumer Reports* appears on-line on computer services like Prodigy, Nexus, Dialog, and Compuserve, meaning that subscribers can get the latest poop on anything that has been tested in the last few years. And Consumers Union's most dramatic findings show up in the pages of newspapers and on the six o'clock news.

For instance, a few years back it was the first to report that the tip-prone Suzuki Samarai might more accurately be called the Kamikaze. In the 1950s, it was the first to warn that fallout from nuclear tests was contaminating milk supplies, a report that led to an international ban on above-ground nuclear tests. By pointing out their simple and durable virtues, *Consumer Reports* helped make the VW Bug and Maytag appliances household words in a time when most manufacturers were sacrificing quality for chrome, fins, gimmicks, and flash. It has exposed entire lines of defective products, including seatbelts and microwave ovens, resulting in higher industry and government standards.

Consumer Reports had its start as a result of muckrakers Stuart Chase, an economist, and Frederick Schlink, an engineer who had once worked for the National Bureau of Standards. In 1927, they published a sarcastic diatribe against shoddy merchandise and dishonest sales techniques called *Your Money's Worth*. It ended with a call for "the principle of buying goods according to impartial scientific test, rather than according to the fanfare and trumpets of higher salesmanship."

A follow-up best-seller called *100,000,000 Guinea Pigs* teamed Schlink and fellow engineer Arthur Kallet in a warning about the everyday health hazards found in every home and store. One typical story noted that a German Army officer committed suicide by swallowing a tubeful of Pebeco brand toothpaste. Schlink and Kallet wryly wrote about his extravagance, in that "a third of a tube would have been enough to do the job."

Before publishing his books, Schlink had started a small consumers' club that met in a basement in White Plains, New York. With his publishing success, he expanded the club into a product-testing agency, Consumers' Research, Inc. Its mimeographed newsletter became a monthly magazine. It grew in size and impact, but Schlink managed to alienate most of his employees. In 1935, nearly all of them, including his former collaborator Kallet, went on strike. Shortly after, they left en masse and started their own organization, Consumers Union.

More militant, skeptical, and pro-union than Consumers' Research had been, the Consumers Union founders granted themselves across-the-board ten-dollars-a-week salaries. These they waived while waiting for subscription money to come in. In *Consumer Reports'* first issue, dated May 1936, they rated only inexpensive things like toothbrushes, cereal, stockings, and milk because they couldn't afford anything more. (This was the beginning of a proud precedent. The Consumers Union still buys all its test subjects, figuring that samples gotten from the manufacturers might be doctored. They have volunteers across the country who make incognito purchases from regular retail outlets. And *Consumer Reports* does not accept advertising of any kind.)

The feisty little magazine went beyond mere product advice. Its second issue, complete with commentary and cartoons, won William Randolph Hearst's undying enmity by blasting his supposedly proconsumer *Good Housekeeping* "Seal of Approval" as nothing more than a hype that benefited no one but his most loyal advertisers. *Good Housekeeping* responded with a blistering attack that accused the Consumers Union of being a communist organization working against honest businessmen and trying to prolong the Depression. The controversy gave *Consumer Reports* much-needed publicity and boosted its circulation from 4,000 to 37,000 in its first year. But advertisers leaned on other publications and more than sixty of them, including *Newsweek* and the *New York Times*, refused the Consumers Union's subscription ads. *Business Week* went so far as to warn its readers against *Consumer Reports'* "organized discontent."

In 1939, the House Un-American Activities Committee, figuring that whatever was bad for General Motors was bad for America, listed the Consumers Union as a subversive organization. The Consumers Union shrugged off the accusation. "If the condemnation of worthless, adulterated, and misrepresented products is a communistic activity," *Consumer Reports* responded in an editorial, "then the Federal Food and Drug

Administration, the Federal Trade Commission, and the American Medical Association must be paid direct from Moscow."

The Consumers Union has been sued for libel dozens of times by corporations. It takes great pride in having never lost or even settled a case. It also refuses to allow its ratings to be used in advertisements. If a company violates its ban, it will first receive a letter from Consumers Union legal counsel—and then thousands of letters from irate readers of *Consumer Reports* after the magazine prints the culprit's name in its "dishonor roll" column. That usually does the trick, but, if necessary, *Consumer Reports* will take the company to court.

In 1990, the Consumers Union moved its forty-two testing labs and 350 employees to new headquarters bought with donations from *Consumer Reports* readers. Most of its testing is done there, though not on cars. They are shipped to Haddam, Connecticut, to be put through their paces on a former drag strip and on hilly, unpaved access roads. "If Michigan had roads like this," says a Consumers Union car tester, "Detroit wouldn't have produced so many poor-handling cars all these decades."

The Yonkers test site is a hum of continuous activity. There are usually six or seven tests going on at any one time. On a typical day, you might find local volunteers taste-testing cookies and brands of cereal. Robots may be putting calculators through their paces, seeing how many times they can add one plus one before the buttons break. Luggage may be tumbling in a giant rotating cylinder. Robot combs may be combing hair conditioner through the disembodied tresses of hair bought from a group of cloistered Italian nuns.

The dishwasher test is typical of Consumers Union's obsessive thoroughness: Dozens of dinner plates and bowls are marked off and caked with identical hard-to-clean messes—chipped beef, evaporated milk, spinach, spaghetti and the like—before being placed into dishwashers. Self-cleaning ovens are coated with "Monster Mash," a concoction that includes tapioca, cheese, lard, grape jelly, cherry pie filling, and tomato sauce. Paper towels are wetted with exactly ten drops of water, stretched across hoops, and tested with lead shot for strength (the winner held over seven pounds, the loser, less than one).

Although Consumers Union buys all its test samples, it recoups some of the cost by selling them afterward to employees. It also publishes a consumer magazine for kids, *Zillions*, that reviews things like bubble gums, video games, and book backpacks.

How Betty Crocker Baked Her Way to the Top

In the 1940s, Betty Crocker was voted the second most well-known woman in America, second only to Eleanor Roosevelt. Not bad for a person who doesn't exist.

Betty was created in 1921, the indirect result of a promotion put on by the Washburn Crosby Company, which milled flour (years later it would change its name to General Mills). The company printed puzzle pieces in a magazine advertisement. The idea was to cut them out and paste them together (the finished puzzle depicted a scene of happy workers loading Gold Medal Flour onto a truck). For everybody who completed the puzzle correctly, the company promised a valuable prize: a pincushion in the shape of a miniature Washburn Crosby flour sack.

Three thousand people sent in entries. That in itself was a surprise. The company had planned for fewer responses and didn't have enough of the pin cushions. When employees began opening the mail, they ran into another unexpected development: A number of respondents sent in questions about baking like "How do you make a one-crust cherry pie?" They clearly expected answers.

Management put out a request to employees and their spouses for copies of their best recipes. Meanwhile, employees began writing out personal responses to each letter. But, they asked, were they supposed to sign their own name at the bottom, or what? Advertising manager Sam Gale came up with a name—Betty, because it was friendly sounding and female, and Crocker in honor of William G. Crocker, a recently retired director of the company. Women employees were invited to submit sample signatures for Betty, and the winning signature went on the bottom of the letters (in fact, it's still in use today).

In 1924, Washburn Crosby bought a local radio station and began presenting the "Betty Crocker Cooking School of the Air" using a member of the station's staff as the voice of Betty. The show became quite popular, so the company expanded it to twelve other stations around the country. Each station had its own Betty Crocker voice, reading scripts from the Crosby home service department back in Minneapolis. In 1927, the "Cooking School" show moved onto the NBC network, where, for the next twenty-four years, it produced more than a million "graduates."

Until 1931, Betty was selling only flour. That changed in 1931 when a Washburn Crosby sales executive stole an idea from a Southern Pacific railroad cook. He had ordered biscuits and was surprised to get them fresh-baked a short time later. He discovered that the chef was using his own premixed dry ingredients that he merely had to add milk to. The executive went back to his office and, with the help of company chemists, invented Bisquick.

In 1936, the company hired an artist named Neysa McMein to paint a portrait of Betty. McMein blended the faces of home service department employees and came up with a midfiftyish, graying, motherly image, which appeared on boxes of Bisquick and Betty Crocker cake mix for the next nineteen years.

It was the first of seven portraits. When Betty was painted again in 1955, the artist lopped about ten years off her earlier image, making her look like one of several TV sitcom moms of the time. Her 1965 portrait lopped another ten years off her age and made her look a bit like Jackie Kennedy. It being the turbulent 1960s, Betty's next update was just three years later, giving her longer hair and an age reduction of another five years. The 1972 Betty took a turn for the uglier, looking inexplicably like Lynda Bird Johnson. The 1980 Betty was roughly twenty-eight, sporting a Lady Di–Dorothy Hamill shortish hairdo.

And then, in 1986, Betty's image took a wrong turn: Betty "Mary Cunningham" Crocker. The only thing she has in common with her predecessors is the trademark red jacket—but this one is a red business suit. Around her neck she has one of those horrendous bows that were once in fashion for a few weeks in 1986 among female MBAs. With her cocked head and noncommittal smile, she appears to be one of those overly ambitious twenty-four year olds who'd do almost anything if it helped her career. She looks like someone who probably eats out every night, whose only cooking has consisted of half-baked plots to take over the company and move all of its jobs to Singapore. As of this writing, the "Ms. Yuppie Scum" Betty is still the company's official symbol, but her replacement is clearly overdue.

How the Goodyear Blimp Got Its Nose in the Air

The Goodyear blimp is one of America's most beloved and enduring corporate symbols. There are actually four of them—one stationed in the East, one in the central states, one in western United States, and one in Europe—and they seem to be ubiquitous, drifting lazily in the sky above every major outdoor event from the World Series and Super Bowl to the Live Aid concert. Much of Goodyear's product differentiation comes from that blimp; it is one thing that keeps the Goodyear name in the consciousness of most people. It's hard to believe that a few decades ago, the Goodyear board came within a few votes of retiring the blimp as "a waste of money"!

Despite the company name, Goodyear was not founded by Charles Goodyear, who in 1839 discovered how to vulcanize rubber. He didn't get rich from his process—in fact, he died penniless in 1860. But when Frank A. Seiberling started a rubber company in Akron, Ohio, in 1898, he decided to name it after the unsung inventor. Some of his motivation may have been to profit from the confusion in having a name that was very similar to another, better established Akron rubber company, the B.F. Goodrich Company, founded twenty-eight years earlier by Benjamin Franklin Goodrich. If so, the ploy worked—the two companies have been confused in the public mind for decades.

It was a good time to get into into the rubber business. Bicycles were the rage and automobiles were about to become the next big thing. Although Goodyear's first primary product lines were bicycle and horse carriage tires, it also manufactured rubber pads for horseshoes, assorted rubber products sold in drug stores, rubber bands, and rubber poker chips. Goodyear produced its first automobile tire in 1901.

Meanwhile, Seiberling hired his first college-educated technician. Paul W. Litchfield, a recent graduate of MIT, was paid $2,500 a year to be factory supervisor, tire designer, rubber compounder, and head of personnel. Like his boss, Litchfield had turn-of-century confidence in technology and American know-how. He kept an eye open for any new application for Goodyear's rubber products. Goodyear began manufacturing airplane tires in 1909, six years after the Wright brothers' first flight, at a time when there were fewer than one hundred airplanes in operation in the United States.

This interest in the potential of aeronautics blossomed into a full-scale obsession. When Litchfield visited Europe in 1910, he looked into European progress in development of airplanes. Litchfield visited the North British Company in Scotland, which had developed a process for spreading rubber over fabric. He traded them the specifications to Goodyear's straight-sided tire for the process's equipment and American rights. North British also threw in two Scottish technicians to run the machines.

Within months, the rubberized cloth was adopted by the Wright brothers (this was back when airplanes were based on kite designs and made of mostly wood and cloth). Within a few years, Goodyear's cloth was used on most airplanes flying in the United States.

The same rubberized fabric turned out to be useful for lighter-than-air craft, although Goodyear's first venture didn't bode well. The dirigible *Akron* was intended to make the first intercontinental flight from the United States to Europe. Its flight began from Atlantic City at daybreak, July 2, 1912, but ended twenty-three minutes later when the ship exploded mysteriously over the ocean. The crew of five was never seen again.

But Goodyear management was still convinced that there was a future for lighter-than-air aircraft, and World War I gave them a chance to prove it. Goodyear produced about one thousand balloons and sixty dirigibles and blimps for observation and reconnaissance. The blimps were particularly useful for moving low over coastal waters and searching out enemy submarines.

By the way, blimps are not the same as dirigibles (sometimes called Zeppelins after their inventor, Count Ferdinand von Zeppelin). The difference is that dirigibles have rigid walls to hold the gas and blimps have flexible ones that maintain their shape from the pressure of helium or hydrogen within.

After the war, the navy pressed ahead with dirigible research. Having seen how well the enemy's dirigibles carried heavy loads, even in conditions of poor visibility, it commissioned the Zeppelin works in Germany to build a dirigible in 1921. They christened it the USS *Los Angeles*. The navy was further impressed when it flew from Germany to New Jersey in eighty-one hours. They asked Goodyear to buy the American rights to the Zeppelin design. The result was the Goodyear-Zeppelin Corporation. In 1926, the Germans finished the Graf Zeppelin, which, over the next nine years, transported 13,110 passengers and covered more than a million miles in a total of 544 trips, including 144 ocean crossings.

Unfortunately, not all Zeppelins were so reliable. In 1930, a British dirigible crashed in France, killing forty-eight of the fifty-four people aboard.

Goodyear's two ships, the *Akron II* and the *Macon*, also went down in tragedy. The *Akron II* crashed off the New Jersey coast, killing seventy-three of the seventy-six people aboard, including Rear Admiral William A. Moffett, chief of the navy's bureau of aeronautics.

A month before, on March 11, 1933, the *Macon* had been christened by Moffett's wife. Two years later, it set course for its home base near San Francisco, but hit a storm and plunged into the sea. Ironically, its base had been recently renamed Moffett Field to honor the deceased real admiral.

The final blow to dirigibles occurred on May 6, 1937, when the German Zeppelin *Hindenburg* burst into flames just seconds before landing in New Jersey. Fewer people died than in the previous disasters—thirty-five of ninety-seven crew and passengers—but, since it took place in front of reporters and newsreel photographers, the image of the disaster was splashed all over the world to great effect.

(For half a century, people have wondered why the Germans used flammable hydrogen in the *Hindenburg* instead of fireproof helium. It was because they had no choice. Helium is actually a fairly rare natural gas, found in abundance only in America. Wary of the Nazis that ruled Germany, the U.S. government had refused to sell them helium, forcing them to use hydrogen.)

While the world pretty much gave up on lighter-than-air travel by the 1930s, Goodyear continued designing and making blimps for research and promotional purposes. In 1929 they had four small ones traveling around the country, each capable of carrying four passengers and a pilot. Goodyear called them the *Pilgrim*, *Puritan*, *Mayflower*, and *Vigilant*, beginning a six-decade-long tradition of naming its blimps after American contenders in the America's Cup international yacht races.

When World War II started, the company built 168 blimps for observation and antisubmarine missions. They patrolled both coasts and accompanied naval vessels. One blimp was the center of a mystery that has never been solved. In the early hours of August 16, 1942, the airship *Ranger* took off from

Treasure Island in San Francisco Bay with a crew of two. It carried two antisubmarine depth bombs. That afternoon, residents of Daly City, down the peninsula from San Francisco, were surprised to see a blimp coming in for a perfect landing in the middle of a residential street.

The blimp was well-stocked with fuel and helium, its batteries were charged, the radio was operating, and emergency life raft and parachutes were on board. Everything seemed to be fine, except for a few small details: The door was open; one depth charge was gone; and both members of the crew were missing. Neither man was ever seen again. The navy never came up with a satisfactory explanation.

An offshoot of Goodyear's blimp works are those giant balloons, as seen in Macy's Thanksgiving Parade. Similar balloons were used to fool the Germans in World War II as the Allies prepared for the D-Day invasion. In 1944, German reconnaissance began reporting huge armadas of boats, tanks, trucks, and artillery that would appear overnight at an English port and then disappear just as suddenly after a few days, reappearing somewhere else a night or two later. Goodyear's balloon designers had produced inflatable replicas of heavy equipment and watercraft. Under cover of darkness, the Allied forces trucked them to a port and inflated them for display the next morning. A few nights later, the models would be deflated and trucked to another port. Thanks in part to this Allied "grand ruse," the Germans reacted in a confused and erratic way in defending the coast of Europe.

After the war, Goodyear bought five of its blimps back from the military (including the *Ranger* of the Daly City mystery) and began using them for promotional purposes. But the company's executives didn't seem to know the value of what it had—in 1958, its board of directors considered grounding the blimps permanently to save operating and maintenance expenses. The plan was stalled by a last-minute plea by Goodyear's publicity director, Robert Lane. To show the blimps' worth, he scheduled a hyperactive six-month marathon tour that sent the *Mayflower* barnstorming the eastern seaboard and generated so much favorable press that the company was convinced to keep it.

The current blimps are the *Eagle*, based in Los Angeles; the *Spirit of Akron*, based in Akron, Ohio; the *Stars and Stripes*, based in Florida; and the *Europa*, based in Rome, Italy.

Some random facts:

• The word "blimp" is credited to Lt. A. D. Cunningham of Britain's Royal Navy Air Service. In 1915, he whimsically flicked his thumb against the inflated wall of an airship and verbally imitated the sound—"Blimp! Blimp!"

• Each Goodyear blimp's light displays consist of 7,650 blue, green, red, and yellow auto tail lights connected to a computer by 80 miles of wiring.

• The blimps are 192 feet long, 59 feet high, and hold 202,700 cubic feet of helium. The helium doesn't leak out quickly like a balloon, but does have to be topped off every four months or so. They have a traveling range of about 500 miles at a cruising speed of 45 to 50 miles per hour. Each blimp has a crew of five pilots, seventeen support members who work on rotating schedules, and a public relations representative.

• Each blimp can carry nine passengers. The seats have no seatbelts.

• The blimps' skin is about as thick as a shirt collar, but it's made of neoprene-impregnated Dacron and is quite tough. It's a good thing, too, since Goodyear reports that their blimps are shot at about twenty times a year. In 1990, a man was arrested and accused of deliberately punching a three-foot hole in the blimp with a radio-controlled model airplane. It leaked a lot of helium, but made it safely home.

• The blimps' first TV sports coverage was an Orange Bowl game in the mid-1960s. Since then, they have been used in about ninety televised events a year. Goodyear doesn't charge TV networks, figuring the publicity generated makes the free service worthwhile. The camera operator shoots from the passenger compartment through an open window from about 400 yards up where he or she can see everything, read the scoreboard, and hear the roar of the crowd. On a calm day, a pilot can hold the blimp virtually still in the air. The hardest sport for the pilots is golf because they have to be careful not to disturb a golfer's shot with engine noise or by casting a sudden shadow over the green.

• The company is secretive about how much the blimps cost, but they acknowledged a few years ago that the annual cost of operating and maintaining four blimps is $6 to $8 million.

• At least one child was reportedly conceived in a Goodyear blimp—Jim Maloney, whose father was a member of the blimp's ground crew in the 1940s. Apparently it had an effect, because Maloney grew up and became one of Goodyear's blimp pilots.

How the Popsicle Got on the Stick

How many things have been invented by eleven-year-old boys? Lots, no doubt. But how many of them would you want to stick in your mouth?

Eleven-year-old Frank Epperson, the story goes, accidentally left a glass of soda pop mix and water on his back porch. The stirring stick was still in it. That night the temperature got well below freezing. Absent-minded Frank went out and found the stick emerging from a frozen block of soft drink. His friends and family were amazed. On that night in 1905, the Popsicle was invented.

You could question the details of the story. On a cold winter day, after all, how many people take a cold drink out to the back porch? How often do eleven year olds mix up a soft drink and then forget to drink it? Isn't it more likely that Epperson had figured out would happen and left the glass outside on purpose? Or even more likely that he simply made the story up years later when his patent application came under question? Hmmm.

Well, regardless, a decade or two later, the very same Frank Epperson was running a lemonade stand at an amusement park in Oakland, California. When a man has to stand and squeeze fruit all day, he starts thinking philosophically. Epperson decided that when life hands you lemonade, you should make Popsicles. He remembered that cold winter night years earlier and decided to blow that lemonade stand, so to speak.

Epperson started making his frozen drinks on a stick and selling them down at the amusement park. He called them

Epsicles, combining his name and "icicles." Nobody seemed too excited by the name, including his own children, who took to calling them "Pop's cycles." Eventually, that name more or less stuck. Popsicles it was.

A few years earlier, a man named Harry Burt had figured out a way to keep the ice cream from falling off. He called the product Good Humor. But he was in a decidedly *bad* humor when he heard that Epperson was trying to patent Popsicles, figuring the similarity was more than coincidental. Burt protested Epperson's patent in 1923. The two eventually reached a compromise: Epperson agreed to make only sherbet or water ice products and leave dairy-based concoctions to Burt. (Years later the two companies merged.)

Popsicles grew very popular in outdoor summer events in the 1920s. When the Great Depression hit, however, the company's profits slipped fast. In response, the company designed the Twin Popsicle we know today, so that two kids could share one nickel Popsicle.

Years ago, Epperson froze each Popsicle in a large test tube using a two-step, several-hour process. Now, though, it takes only about eight minutes. The molds sit in supercooled brine, and the liquid formula is squirted into them. The sticks are stuck in when the liquid thickens enough to hold them up. After freezing, each mold is heated slightly. The hardened Popsicle is pulled out of it and dipped in water, which freezes and gives the Popsicle a glossy sheen.

Popsicles are offered in about three dozen different flavors, but the top three best-selling flavors are the traditional orange, cherry, and grape.

Reader's Digest:
A Condensed History

It's easy to think of the *Reader's Digest* as an anachronism, a Norman Rockwell painting set in type, a remnant of another time and place when all true Americans were Caucasians living in small towns, holding a steadfast faith in God, Republicanism, the Flag, a strong defense, monogamous heterosexual marriages with rigid roles, and the benefits of hard work.

Yet, if that's true, there must be an awful lot of time-warped white middle-Americans worldwide. Because every month, *Reader's Digest* publishes *28 million copies* in over 170 countries and seventeen languages, reaching about 100 million readers all over the globe. A quarter of all American homes subscribe, and not just smalltown folks: More people in New York read the *Digest* than the *Times*; more Bostonians read it than the *Boston Globe*; and more San Franciscans read it than the *San Francisco Chronicle*.

Picking up a copy, with its mix of reprints and original stories about health, politics, religion, positive thinking, inspiration, heroic true-life dramas, and humor, gives only a small clue to its wide and diverse appeal. A casual reader could imagine that it would might do moderately well in the marketplace. But 28 million copies? Unfathomable. So maybe it's not surprising that the idea of *Reader's Digest* was originally rejected by every major publisher in the country.

It all started with a Midwestern minister's son named DeWitt Wallace who was kicked out of high school in 1907 at age seventeen. He banged around the country for a year before enrolling at the University of California, from which he promptly dropped out.

Wallace went to work at his uncle's bank in Colorado, where he began reading voraciously. He started keeping a card file summarizing the better articles he had run across. After a few years, he moved back to St. Paul and got a job writing promotional literature for a magazine called *The Farmer*. One day, while looking at government pamphlets, he realized that most farmers had no idea that the helpful information existed. Wallace put together a pamphlet describing available publications and set out in a car to sell it to banks in rural areas for goodwill distribution to their customers. He sold 100,000 copies around the Midwest. One night, while lying awake in a Montana bunkhouse, he began thinking about doing something similar for a general readership.

In 1916, he went back to St. Paul to work as a mail-order manager for a greeting card company. Bored with his job, he immediately enlisted in the army when World War I broke out. In France, half his battalion was killed and Wallace was hit with shrapnel in the neck, nose, abdomen, and lungs. He spent the rest of his stint in a French hospital.

While there, he filled the time by reading American magazines. The writing style at the time was more flowery than now (in part because those were slower, more literary times—and in part because most writers were paid by the word). As an experiment, Wallace began rewriting some of the articles, shrinking them in length while retaining as many of the author's original words as possible. He came to the conclusion that most could be shortened by at least 75 percent without losing their flavor or meaning.

By the time Wallace returned to the States in 1919, he had perfected the technique of "condensing" popular literature. In

January 1920 he put together a sample copy of what he was already calling *The Reader's Digest*. It was remarkably similar to what the *Digest* is now, containing thirty-one shortened articles "of enduring value and interest," reprinted from other publications with titles like "The Art of Opening a Conversation," "How to Regulate Your Weight," "What People Laugh At," and "America's Most Popular Crime."

He had several hundred copies of the dummy printed up and sent them off to publishers all over the country. All he wanted was for one of them to pick up the idea and hire him to be its editor. Instead, he got rejection letters from every one of them. A few included reasons: The editor of the *Woman's Home Companion* wrote to say that the magazine only carried articles because it was necessary to attract advertisers, so why would she be interested in a magazine in which articles were the whole point? Only William Randolph Hearst was even faintly encouraging—he wrote that the *Digest* might in time hit a circulation peak of 300,000 subscribers, but that his company wouldn't be interested in a venture that small.

Wallace had spent all his money on the prototypes and was bitterly discouraged. He gave up and turned his attention to wooing a childhood friend named Lila Bell Acheson, who was working as a social worker for the YMCA.

Wallace took a job in Pittsburgh doing promotional work for Westinghouse, but was fired shortly afterward. Acheson married him anyway, and encouraged him to publish his magazine himself. He started soliciting potential subscribers one by one from lists of doctors, nurses, professors, and teachers. Over the next several months, Wallace invented the personalized direct-pitch mailing that the *Digest* used successfully years later when computers became available: "Dear John Smith, How are things there at 1313 Mockingbird Lane . . . ?"

The only problem was that this was decades before computers made the job easy. For four months, Wallace himself typed the individual opening page of the mailings, describing his new publication, offering a money-back guarantee, and asking for a subscription to it. Provisional subscriptions and funds began dribbling in.

When the Wallaces had received $5,000 in subscriptions, they borrowed another $1,300 and published five thousand copies of *The Reader's Digest*, February 1922, Volume 1, Number 1. It ran to sixty-two pages with no illustrations, no color, a cover that was the same white stock as the inner pages, and no advertising (the *Digest* would continue its no-ads policy for thirty-three years).

The Wallaces moved to New York and rented a small Greenwich Village office under a speakeasy at 1 Minetta Lane. When the first five thousand copies came back from the printer, the Wallaces hired some barflies from upstairs and some women from a "community club" down the street to wrap and address them.

They mailed Volume 1 out that night, excited but scared. They had blown all the money they had collected for one-year subscriptions, and then some, and had published only one issue. If any significant number of subscribers decided to take them up on their money-back guarantee, they were ruined. In fact, they'd be bankrupt if they didn't get a whole new bunch of subscribers quickly to pay for the next issue.

To save money, they sublet one room of their apartment and waited. To their relief, nobody canceled. More importantly, word-of-mouth started bringing in a steady stream of new subscriptions. Within six months, they had seven thousand subscribers.

Feeling cramped by the piles of magazines and correspondence, the Wallaces rented a cottage in a small town with the absurdly euphonious name of Pleasantville, where *Reader's*

Digest headquarters remain to this day. Acheson (who kept her maiden name for several years) read articles and marked candidates for inclusion, Wallace made the final selections, condensed the articles in longhand on legal paper, and arranged for permissions from publishers. By 1925, circulation was up to 16,000, and they began hiring a small staff. By 1929, circulation was 200,000 and climbing, reaching 1,450,000 by 1936. In 1949, they began Reader's Digest Books, offering condensed versions of popular literature.

The Wallaces continued at the top of the masthead for the next five decades. They became incredibly rich and reportedly gave away over $100 million to charitable, educational, religious, arts, and political organizations. Both died in their nineties in the early 1980s.

How Spam Resulted from Too Many Cold Shoulders

Margaret Thatcher ate it for Christmas dinner in 1943. Nikita Khrushchev credited it for keeping the Soviet army alive during World War II. Monty Python wrote a song about it. GIs in World War II joked that it was "ham that flunked its physical." Its manufacturer calls it "the Rodney Dangerfield of luncheon meat—It don't get no respect."

We're talking Spam, ladies and gentlemen, also known as "mystery meat" or (to quote those Python boys) "Spam Spam Spam Spam / Lovely Spam, oh wonderful Spam. . . ." It is much maligned, but much eaten as well, accounting for 75 percent of all luncheon meat sales in this country. Spam is especially popular in Hawaii, which has the highest per capita Spam consumption rate in the nation. (And, let the record show, the highest life expectancy in the nation as well—eighty-four and eighty years for women and men respectively. Coincidence? We think not. Perhaps sodium compounds preserve more than pork products.)

In Korea, Spam is thought of as an imported luxury item, a part of the good life. A can of it is often given as a present on a date, or to coworkers and business associates, and even to newlyweds. Koreans often fry it with a peppery cabbage dish called *kimchi* or roll it up into *kimpap*, a sushilike Spam item made with rice and seaweed.

But why was Spam invented in the first place? Because of a surplus of pig shoulders. Every meat processor runs into the problem of what to do with the parts of the animal that are less popular than others. Pork shoulders, for example, aren't meaty enough to sell as ham, and aren't fatty enough to slice into bacon. Seeing pork shoulders piling up in the coolers of the George A. Hormel Company in 1937 gave one of its executives an idea. Why not chop the meat up, add some spices and meat from other parts of the pig, and form it into small ham-like loaves? Put it in a can and fill the excess space with gelatin from the pig's leftover skin and bones—you could probably keep the meat edible for months without refrigeration.

They tried it. It worked. Hormel's Spiced Ham quickly found a niche in the market. It was inexpensive, savory, convenient, and it didn't need refrigeration.

Other packers, also plagued with a surplus of leftover pig parts, began issuing their own "Spiced Hams." Hormel offered a prize of $100 for a name that would differentiate its product from the imitators. A brother of one of its workers contracted "Spiced Ham" and got Spam.

Spam was bolstered by an ad campaign that showed how it could be served morning, noon, and night and by the sixty-strong traveling Hormel Girls ("Spam, Spam, Spam, Spam / Hormel's new miracle meat in a can / Tastes fine, saves time / If you want something grand, ask for Spam . . . " sung awkwardly to the tune of "My Bonnie Lies Over the Ocean").

When World War II came, Spam's price, portability, and shelf life made it a ubiquitous staple of every GI's diet. The gospel according to Spam was also spread by American aid packages to its allies. Although many GIs swore that they'd never eat the stuff again (even Dwight Eisenhower complained about too much Spam in army messes), they apparently got a craving once they got out of uniform, because Spam did booming business immediately after the war. Even now, 228 cans of Spam are eaten every minute of the day.

Customer Service

It isn't that we build such bad cars; it's that they are such lousy customers.
—Charles F. Kettering, president and chairman of the board,
General Motors, 1925–1949

Do not use the word "contract." Use the word "agreement." And don't ask the prospect if he wants the lot. Ask him a question and write the answer on your agreement. Ask, "What is your correct name, sir? What is your correct mailing address?" And so on through the agreement. Remember, if he has let you fill out the agreement, he has bought. *Okay, what do you do when you get to the bottom? Don't ask him to sign. You know what's wrong with the word "sign"? You have been taught all your life to read every word, be careful, beware, don't sign anything. So you ask him to* okay *the agreement. He won't* sign *it, but he will* okay *it.*
—Real estate sales memo quoted in
The Great Land Hustle by James O. Foote

Let the buyer beware; that covers the whole business. You cannot wet-nurse people from the time they are born until the time they die. They have got to wade in and get stuck, and that is the way men are educated and cultivated.
—Henry Havemeyer, American Sugar Refining Company,
arguing against consumer protection laws

Celestial Seasonings: Steeped in the 1960s

It wasn't so long ago that when you said "tea," it meant only Lipton's in a bag. Herb teas? Just a few decades ago, not too many people in this country had even heard of them. All that changed with Morris J. "Mo" Siegel.

Siegel, an unreconstructed hippie, learned about herb teas mostly by trial and error. In 1971, he, his wife, Peggy, and two friends, John Wyek Hay and Lucinda Zeisling, started gathering herbs from the hillsides around Boulder, Colorado. They laid the leaves onto old screen doors in the sun to dry, and then sewed them into hand-sewn muslin bags. In the summer of 1971, they were able to sell their entire crop to a local health food store.

Next summer, they borrowed $5,000 from a friend, sold the Siegels' VW Bug, and talked Hay's mother into cosigning a loan for another $5,000. The friends moved their operation into an old barn outside Boulder. It was a time of groovy, cosmic nicknames and Zeisling's was "Celestial." Liking the sound of it, the partners named the company after her.

That year, Siegel came up with a hibiscus and rose hip blend that had a sharp and pleasing flavor and a natural bright red color. He called it Red Zinger. His timing was good—food was becoming a counterculture issue as hippies, who once scarfed down burgers, were suddenly gravitating to natural foods, vegetarianism, and other "alternative" diets.

The Red Zinger name (reminiscent of "Screaming Yellow Zonkers," the trippy snack food of the late 1960s), the tangy flavor, and the promise of healthy ingredients were exactly what the bells and patchouli crowd had in mind. Siegel designed a box that was bright, psychedelic, and covered with aphorisms like:

"I hold that while a man exists, it is his duty to improve not only his own condition, but to assist in ameliorating mankind."
—Abraham Lincoln

"We are the music-makers, and we are the dreamers of dreams, wandering by lone sea breakers, and sitting by desolate streams; world-losers and world-forsakers on whom the pale moon gleams: Yet we are the movers and shakers of the world forever, it seems." —Arthur O'Shaughnessy

Red Zinger and Celestial's other teas started moving off the shelves ... first from health food stores, then from the local Safeway. By 1974, Celestial Seasonings' sales exceeded $1 million.

Up to that time, traditional teamakers considered herb teas to be nothing more than soggy weeds in hot water. When it became clear that herb teas were cutting into their market, their first reaction wasn't to compete—it was to go crying to the government. They found an obscure ruling from 1897 that made it illegal to call anything a "tea" unless it was made of Camellia sirensis, the tea plant, and petitioned the government to enforce it. When that ploy didn't work, they began bringing out their own lines, often imitating Celestial Seasonings' whimsical names and packaging.

In 1984, Siegel sold Celestial out, in every sense of the word, to the giant cheese and salad dressing company, Kraft, Inc. Taking his portion of the $36 million Kraft paid, Siegel went off to find himself by flying to every major country before he turned thirty-eight. "I got to South Africa and, strangely enough, I wanted to kiss the soil because it was my last country," he told an interviewer. "There was kind of like this huge emptiness that also hit the same week."

His existential angst resulted in Earth Wise, a company he founded in 1990 to distribute biodegradable detergents, recycled trash bags, and other environmentally conscious items. The employees of his old company, meanwhile, had their own existential angst to deal with. They had to adapt to the Kraft corporate culture, which looked askance at the no-time-clock, shoes-and-shirt-optional operation that Siegel had founded.

Kraft instituted a dress code and other trappings of modern corporate life. It also required Celestial to do serious, expensive market research before releasing a tea. This was in marked contrast to Celestial's standard methodology of inviting church groups and ladies' clubs for tea tastings—and actually charging them $3.50 a head for the privilege. Kraft also began drawing up plans for Celestial Seasonings salad dressings and packaged spices.

It finally became clear on both sides that Kraft would be better off without Celestial, and vice versa. If Celestial's founding had been a microcosm of the early 1970s, its "liberation" from Kraft was typical of the late 1980s.

First, demonstrating corporate bonehead thinking, Kraft tried to sell the line to Celestial's arch rival, Lipton, in 1988. Another competitor, R.C. Bigelow Teas, sued to block the sale on antitrust grounds. While that suit languished in the courts, Kraft became the target of a hostile takeover by tobacco giant Philip Morris, Inc.

In fear of being crushed in this clash of titans, Celestial management turned to an investment firm, Vestar Capital Partners, Inc., which consisted of seven leveraged buyout experts from Boston. Vestar agreed to provide funds to offer to buy Celestial. Kraft, under pressure and needing capital to stave off Philip Morris, agreed to sell Celestial to them for $60 million.

Celestial, now saddled with a strapping debt, hired Mo Siegel back again as chairman and chief executive. Siegel and Vestar decided to take the company public in 1993, retaining 31 percent of it for themselves, another 20 percent for their employees, and selling the rest for $35 million.

Meanwhile, they dismantled the time clocks, went back to their old dress code, and began inviting ladies' clubs to the tasting rooms again.

How Levi's Moved from a Miner to a Major Fashion Item

What is so essential as blue jeans? Yet, for most of their history, Levi's were considered working-class garments and frowned upon by parents, educators, and other members of the bourgeoisie. That started changing with the Westerns of the 1950s, where stars such as James Dean in *Giant* showed that even cowboys look good in the blues. By the proletariat-chic 1960s, denims (especially when beat up, bleached, torn and/or patched) were on everybody. The 1970s brought forth the oxymoron of designer jeans—denim trousers that cost several times more than dress slacks.

Levi's jeans started with a boy named Loeb Strauss, born in Bavaria in 1829. After his father died of consumption in 1845, his mother decided that there was no future for her children growing up Jewish in anti-Semitic Bavaria. In 1847, Loeb moved with his mother and two sisters to the golden promise of America, where he changed his name to Levi because it "sounded more American."

Strauss's two older brothers had arrived a few years earlier and started a business selling dry goods in New York City. Strauss began learning the business, and in 1848 traveled to Kentucky to earn his living as a traveling peddler, schlepping fabrics, threads, pins, needles, hooks, buttons, ribbons, combs, and scissors from town to town.

Strauss carried his goods on his back with the hope of someday joining the more established peddlers who used a horse-drawn wagon, and then eventually settled down to a store somewhere. (Sometimes this last transition happened when their wagons broke down or their horses suddenly died.) Strauss peddled his wares on foot for several years. Then he succumbed to gold fever.

It was 1849, and gold had been discovered in California. Tens of thousands of laborers, lawyers, teachers, clerks, and farmers made the trek to try getting rich in the gold fields. Twenty-four-year-old Levi Strauss thought he could get rich, too, but not by digging. The influx of people had created shortages of everyday things and jacked prices up. Apples that would cost a nickel in New York sold for fifty cents in California. A fifteen dollar wagon could fetch over $100. Strauss loaded merchandise from his brothers' store onto a ship going around the tip of South America.

Strauss arrived in San Francisco after a five-month journey and found a great demand for the sewing supplies he brought. One account has it that his ship was met by eager merchants in rowboats who bought everything but a roll of tent canvas before the ship had even docked. When he tried to sell the roll, somebody told him, "Canvas, hell. You shoulda' brought pants. Pants don't wear worth a hoot in the diggin's," so Strauss brought the canvas to a tailor and had stiff but sturdy pants sewn from the brown fabric. They sold out in a flash.

Strauss sent word back to New York to send more canvas. Meanwhile, he salvaged sails from among the seven hundred ships in the harbor that sailors had abandoned to dig for gold. (The city eventually sank them into the mud and built boardwalks over them.)

Levi and his brother-in-law David opened a dry goods shop and Levi continued making work clothes out of whatever strong materials came in on the latest merchant ship. Levi peddled pants and other dry goods in mining camps and towns with names like Rough and Ready, Bedbug, Henpeck City, and Groundhog's Glory. He saw firsthand how mining was particularly hard on trousers because of the miners' continuous squatting, kneeling, and stuffing pockets with ore. He learned from the miners that canvas chafed unbearably (most miners didn't wear underwear); they preferred pants made from a flexible but sturdy cotton fabric from Nîme, France, that came in bundles labeled *"serge de Nîme,"* which they read as "denim." Strauss found that indigo was the most popular color because it hid dirt stains.

In 1853, Strauss started Levi Strauss and Company to make and market denim pants full time, using what he had learned from talking to miners in the gold country. But the company still hadn't licked the pocket problem. Miners complained that their tools and ore samples ripped the fabric too easily. Strauss couldn't come up with a satisfactory solution, but a tailor in Reno, Nevada, did. Jacob Davis, a Latvian immigrant, had been given an order for work clothes from a woman who complained that her husband's pockets always tore through. He chose his heaviest twill and then had an idea: Why not use rivets on the pockets to reinforce them? The rivets worked. Davis started making riveted work clothes, selling two hundred pairs of pants in eighteen months.

Davis knew he had a good idea, and he wanted to file a patent on his idea. His wife, however, threatened to leave him if he spent $68 on a patent fee. So he wrote to the Levi Strauss Company and offered to share his idea, if Strauss would finance the patent. He sent along two samples of his pants, one made of duck and the other of blue denim, with this letter:

> The secratt of them pents is the rivits that I put in these Pockets and I found the demand so large that I cannot make them up fast enough. I charge for the Duck $3.00 and the Blue

$2.50 a pear. My nabors are getting yalouse of these success and unless I secure it by Patent Papers it will soon become a general thing. Everybody will make them up and thare will be no money in it.

Therefore Gentlemen, I wish to make you a Proposition that you should take out the Latters Patent in my name as I am the inventor of it, the expense of it will be about $68 all complit. . . . The investment for you is but a trifle compaired with the improvement in all Coarse Clothing. I use it in all Blankit Clothing such as Coats, Vests and Pents, and you will find it a very salable article at a much advenst rate. . . .

While the idea was simple, it had a huge effect on sales. In the first year, Levi sold 21,600 riveted pants and coats to miners, cowboys, lumberjacks, and farmers throughout the West.

The rivet on the fly, by the way, was eventually removed after the company received dozens of hot, testy letters complaining that the rivet was a painfully good conductor of heat when the wearer crouched in front of a campfire. The rivets on the back pockets were first covered, then replaced with reinforced stitching, because of complaints about scratched saddles and furniture.

Levi Strauss grew to be a large company with the reputation of good employee relations and moderately progressive social policies. But that wasn't always the case. In this country, demagoguery and hysteria seems to arise every few decades about immigrants. During the anti-Chinese frenzy of the 1800s, Levi Strauss advertised that "Our riveted goods are made up in our Factory, under our direct supervision, and by WHITE LABOR only."

The claim, used until the end of the century, was not only revolting, but untrue as well. While Levi's sewing was done by sixty white women working for three dollars a day, the fabric cutting was done by a Chinese man. The company repeatedly tried to replace him, but could find no white laborer who was able to do the job.

Over the decades, the company has improved on this score. During World War II, it was among the first to hire African-American workers in its factories, and even in the South refused to keep black workers segregated or limited to low-paying jobs. The company has developed affirmative action programs for minorities and women, and has earned a reputation for treating its employees better than most big corporations.

How the Marlboro Man Got a Sex Change

Did you know that the typical Marlboro smoker, now personified by the rugged cowboys who puff on cigarettes while roping steers, was once a woman? But it wasn't the cowboys who were transsexuals—it was the cigarettes.

Marlboro was born in 1924 as one of the first women's cigarettes. In previous decades, the idea of marketing cigarettes to women was about as taboo then as marketing them to eight year olds is today (ask cartoony Joe Camel about the sticky problems with that one). But with the Suffragettes and the "anything goes" 1920s, women decided that there was no reason they couldn't develop the same filthy habits as men had (the health issues, although known to researchers, were not yet part of public consciousness).

Still, it was a tricky sell. Advertisers had to somehow convince the women that stained teeth, foul breath, and addictive cravings, not to mention that dry, heaving morning cough, were somehow genteel and ladylike. Philip Morris decided that their brand needed to have a classy, sophisticated name. Winston Churchill was in the news at the time, and it was being reported that he was related to the Earl of Marlborough. Philip Morris marketers liked the sound of the Marlborough name, but didn't think it looked good on the pack. They lopped off the "ugh" and came up with Marlboro.

In the 1920s, the Marlboro campaign was based around how ladylike the new cigarette was. They painted a red band around the filter to hide those unattractive lipstick stains, calling them "Beauty Tips to Keep the Paper from Your Lips."

They called Marlboro the "Mild as May" cigarette for women and added a tone of snobbishness—"Discerning feminine taste is now confirming the judgment of masculine connoisseurs in expressing unanimous preference for the Aristocrat of Cigarettes. . . ." The brand developed a small following— enough to keep it alive, but not enough to be called a great success.

Two decades later, Philip Morris decided to "reposition" the brand to fit a new market niche—men who were afraid of dying from lung cancer but too macho to admit it. Here's what happened. In the early 1950s, scientists published a major, well-publicized study linking smoking to lung cancer. This was the "smoking gun" that the cigarette companies had been dreading for years. In 1953, for the first time, cigarette consumption dipped in the United States.

The cigarette companies moved fast. Then, like now, they pursued a contradictory strategy: claiming that the studies were "inconclusive" on cigarette safety while simultaneously implying that their brands were somehow "safer" than those other, more dangerous, brands. The brands that were suffering most were their nonfilter brands. Filter cigarettes were perceived by smokers as safer, but up to that point filter cigarettes had been marketed to only women. Many men now wanted a filtered brand, figuring it was safer, but were afraid they'd be subjected to public ridicule if they switched to a woman's brand.

Cigarette manufacturers had long resisted pushing filter cigarettes to men, in part because they thought filters implied that smoke was unpleasant or dangerous. Now, though, they started seeing a silver lining in so doing. Filtered cigarettes were more profitable because the filter material was cheaper than a comparable amount of tobacco. Besides, filters screened out some of the smoke's harshness, which meant they could get by with a cheaper grade of tobacco.

Philip Morris decided to give Marlboro a sex change operation. The company hired Chicago advertising executive Leo Burnett to do the surgery.

Burnett's specialty was cute advertising characters like the Jolly Green Giant, the Keebler Elves, the lonely Maytag Repairman, Charlie the Tuna, Poppin' Fresh, and Morris the Cat. When he thought about defeminizing Marlboros, he decided to use a series of the most testosterone-laced images he could think of.

He intended to present a series of hunky, sweaty sea captains, weight lifters, adventurers, war correspondents, construction workers, Marines, and the like. The cowboy was his first image of the series. But Philip Morris wasn't sure about the campaign. It hired a research company that came back with the alarming report that there were only three thousand full-time cowboys in the entire United States. How do you expect men working in a downtown office building to relate to an image like that?

Burnett had to do some fast talking, and he eventually convinced the company to try the cowboy. The campaign worked. In one year, Marlboro zoomed from a marginal presence, capturing less than 1 percent of the market, to the fourth best-selling brand. The company decided to forget the sea captains and soldiers and stick with cowboys.

Burnett's first set of cowboys were professional models, some of whom had never been a horse before. That led to a series of embarrassing gaffes that left cowpokes-in-the-know snickering. For example, an early ad showed a cowboy's legs in close-up: His blue jeans were well-worn, his hand-tooled boots were scuffed in all the right places ... but his spurs were upside-down. After that, the agency started recruiting real cowboys from places like Texas and Montana for their ads.

In 1955, the agency added a trademark tattoo to their cowboy's hand. One model observed after a photo shoot that they had spent three minutes making up his face—and three hours painting the tattoo. In 1962, Burnett's agency bought the rights to *The Magnificent Seven* theme and added words to it for their TV ads ("Come to where the flavor is . . . Come to Marlboro Country").

Since then, the Marlboro Man has been among the most successful campaigns ever, keeping the cigarette at or near the top of the heap for years. When cigarette ads were banned in 1971, the cowboy made a smooth transition to print and billboards since he never said anything anyway. He continued squinting off into the distance with that self-absorbed expression that addicts have when contemplating their next fix.

Everyone seems to love the cowboy. The image seems to work as well at convincing women to smoke Marlboros as men. It also works well with blacks and Hispanics. That's ironic—even though many real cowboys have been black or Hispanic, all the Marlboro men have been Caucasian. Best of all for the company (which has to replace all those dying dying-breed customers), the cowboy has worked as a role model with kids and teens as well, making Marlboro the number-one starter brand.

The popularity of the cowboy image has led to antismoking parodies as well. In France, Philip Morris sued an antismoking group that used a cowboy model to deliver an antismoking message, claiming trademark infringement. Philip Morris won a pyrrhic victory—a judgment of 1 franc instead of the $3 million they had asked for—but at least they got the ads off the air.

The real cowboy models, meanwhile, have periodically embarrassed the company by dying like desperadoes from smoking-related diseases like lung cancer, emphysema, and strokes. There's some evidence that the Marlboro man may be deemphasized in future Marlboro promotions. In 1993, in what industry analysts suggested is an attempt to keep novice smokers coming, Philip Morris lowered the price of Marlboros for the first time and presented a non-cowboy promotion, the Marlboro Adventure Team, in which smokers accrue "Adventure Miles" for every pack smoked. These can be turned in for Marlboro-logo sports equipment (instead of infinitely more practical Marlboro-logo oxygen tanks, wheelchairs, and hospital beds).

Smoke Screen

Cigarettes are not addictive.
> —Brennan Dawson, Tobacco Institute, 1994

I think we overuse the word "addictive." I think smoking can be a habit.
> —Brennan Dawson, Tobacco Institute, 1991

It's always been our policy that young people shouldn't smoke.
> —Brennan Dawson, Tobacco Institute, 1991

There is no science behind the accusation that advertising causes smoking initiation.
> —Thomas Lauria, Tobacco Institute, 1991

This attempt to ban smoking is an example of social engineering on a vast scale. Such massive intervention in the private lives and choices of one quarter of our adult population recalls the extremism of Prohibition, the last national crusade against a supposed social evil.
> —Charles Whitley, Tobacco Institute, 1990

If I saw or thought that there were any evidence whatsoever that conclusively proved that, in some way, tobacco was harmful to people, and I believed it in my heart and my soul, then I would get out of the business and I wouldn't be involved in it. Honestly, I have not seen one piece of medical evidence that has been presented by anybody, anywhere that absolutely, totally said that smoking caused the disease or created it. I believe this. I'm sitting here talking to you with an extremely clear conscience.
> —Gerald H. Long, president of R.J. Reynolds Tobacco Company, May 19, 1986, as quoted in the *Washington Times*

It's part of the whole anti-business movement, the Green Movement. If you think it's bad here, it's even worse in Europe. People have more time to think these days, and so they're more and more critical of everything. Look how critical they are of governments. And there's this health-consciousness movement running through the world.

—John Dollisson, vice president of corporate affairs,
Philip Morris, explaining the
antismoking movement

Gosh, we're awed at how a story can be told and retold by the anti-cigarette people, and how little attention is given in the press to claims for cigarettes.

—James C. Bowling, assistant to the president, Philip Morris

I think that if it were ever conclusively shown that there was some connection between smoking and, say, lung cancer, most ad agencies would not be advertising cigarettes. But it's easy to get stampeded, and the tobacco industry is being very much maligned. . . . The fact is that I have never met a finer group in my life than the people in the tobacco industry. . . . And tobacco has given pleasure to an awful lot of people. You should never act on hunches, suspicions, and stir-ups.

—Henry Pattison, account executive for the Philip Morris
Company at the Benton and Bowles Agency, 1969

Just what the doctor ordered.

—Ad, L & M cigarettes, 1956

Lothesome to the eye, hatefull to the Nose, harmfull to the braine, dangerous to the Lungs, and in the stinking fume thereof, nearest resembling the horrific Stigian smoke of the pit that is bottomless.

—King James I, in a decree banning tobacco
from his kingdom, 1604

How a Radio Comedian Made Colonel Sanders Turn Chicken

It was midlife crisis and an observation by cowboy philosopher Will Rogers that turned Harlan Sanders's life around.

In 1930, Rogers observed on his radio show, "Let me tell you something: Life begins at forty." The line has since become a cliché, but at the time it was new and it made a big impression on Harlan Sanders. Sanders had coincidentally just turned forty and was in the throes of a deep depression. Looking back at his life, he had been a failure at everything he had tried, and didn't have much reason to believe things were going to get better.

Sanders had dropped out of school at age fourteen and hit the road. He tried being a farmhand but didn't like it. He became a streetcar conductor at age sixteen, but got fired a few weeks later. He tried the army but hated it and got discharged after a year. He tried blacksmithing and couldn't make a living at it.

Finally, he found a job he liked—as a locomotive fireman for the Southern Railroad. Thinking he was finally settled, he married his girlfriend. A few months later, she announced that she was pregnant—on the same day he was getting ready to tell her he'd been fired again.

He started job-hunting. One day he came home and found that his pregnant wife had sold all of their possessions and moved back to her parents' house. He found a succession of railroad jobs and began studying law by a correspondence course, but eventually dropped out of that, too. He sold tires. He sold insurance. He ran a ferryboat. He worked as a secretary. He thought he would always be a failure.

Will Rogers's observation jolted Sanders out of his passivity. He decided to try something completely new as his forty-plus life began. He opened a little gas station in Kentucky on U.S. 25, the main highway to Florida from "up North." He added a small luncheonette and started making food for travelers.

Sanders realized that his cuisine was nothing special. He began concocting new recipes. Trying to fix his tasteless fried chicken, he started messing around with seasonings. After weeks of messing around, he came up with his personal Holy Grail—the Harlan Sanders Kentucky Fried Chicken Secret Recipe with Eleven Herbs and Spices.

Sanders began serving it out of his gas station. His fried chicken started getting famous among locals and frequent travelers. The governor of Kentucky, Ruby Laffon, even made him a Kentucky Colonel in 1935 in honor of his contribution to roadside cuisine. The honorary title wasn't that big a deal—Kentucky colonels were pretty much a dime-a-dozen—but Harlan liked the sound of Colonel Sanders and started using the title on a regular basis.

For the first time in his life, Sanders began feeling like a success. He started making a pretty good living. Things went pretty well for a decade, but then the highway department built a new road for interstate travelers. It missed Sanders's gas station by a good seven miles. Suddenly the river of cars going by his luncheonette slowed to a trickle.

Still, a few loyal customers continued to drive out of their way to have some of his once-famous chicken. Sanders was able to eke out a living. Years went by. Then something else happened that jarred Sanders into action again. He turned sixty-five and got his first Social Security check.

Feeling anything but socially secure, he decided to use the money from his first check to franchise his fried chicken recipe to other restaurants. He traveled around the region, demonstrating his chicken to potential investors and restaurateurs.

Several restaurants took him up on the deal. He didn't charge anything upfront to franchise his recipe—he just provided the mysterious secret spice mix and asked that the licensees send him five cents for every chicken they dismembered and sold, completely on the honor system.

"It was slow for a while," he recalled later, "but then it began to take hold. Eventually I began to realize how Mr. Woolworth built up such a big business with his five-and-dime stores. Those nickels really add up when they're rolling in."

So what's in the secret mix? Well, only a few people know. When the Colonel started franchising, he hired two different spice companies, each to put together half the spices so that neither could know the complete recipe. But when "fast-food detective" Gloria Pitzer was on a Dallas talk show, she got an on-air call from the Colonel who said that all the ingredients could be picked up at a normal grocery store. She told him she had created a taste-alike facsimile of his recipe consisting of three cups flour, one tablespoon paprika, two envelopes Lipton Cup-A-Soup, and two envelopes Seven Seas Italian Dressing. His reaction? "Now you're cookin'."

In 1964, the Colonel sold his business to some entrepreneurs from Louisville; in 1971, they sold out to liquor manufacturer Heublin, Inc., which was caught up in the diversification and conglomeration fad of the time. The Colonel was not happy with what they did to his recipes. He had been hired by the company to personify the product and keep his opinions to himself. But the Colonel had lived long enough to call a spade a spade, and, despite his well-paying figurehead position, he let his displeasure be known. In interviews with journalists, he called the new "extra crispy" chicken "a damn fried doughball stuck on some chicken," and the conglomerate's gravy "pure wallpaper paste. . . . They've had fourteen years doin' it the wrong way. Good gravy's the essence of chicken, don't you know. You make the gravy the way it's supposed to be, and you'll throw out the chicken and eat the gravy." He visited an outlet in New York City and declared its food "the worst fried chicken I've ever seen," and added with a sigh, "Everything's just got too doggone commercial."

Sanders died in 1980 at the age of ninety. In 1993, the company started offering a rotisserie chicken. Their ads said that "legend has it" that it was the Colonel's own recipe, lost and rediscovered. In posthumous response, you can almost hear the Colonel's voice echoing through the mists of time. In another interview, he reacted bitterly to a brochure the company put out called "The Colonel's Other Recipes."

"Now you'll see a lot of 'Colonel Sanders's recipes' that I never had anything to do with," he said, pointing to a photo of a platter of shiny chicken pieces. Above it, the subhead read, "A down-home favorite. This authentic recipe was served by the Colonel at the Sanders's neighborhood barn dances years ago. . . ."

"That barbecued chicken," then-living legend Harlan Sanders said with emphasis, "now that's a bunch of shit."

How Muzak Invented Mood-Elevator Music

When's the last time you listened to Muzak? What song was playing? What, you don't remember? That's good. You're not supposed to remember. In fact, if it's working "right," you're not supposed to even notice it. It's all tied into a theory of music as ambience, as environment, as something meant to surround you and change your mood without your noticing. With Muzak, you're supposed to be happier, more optimist, and (most important) more *productive*—without even knowing why!

If you want to make Muzak's 174 franchisers and 200,000 subscribers mad, call it background music or elevator music. *They* call it functional music or (since the first Earth Day?) environmental music. It's all tied into a theory called Stimulus Progression. To quote company literature: "Each segment plays music on an ascending curve during descending periods of the industrial work curve." In other words, they play peppy music at the times when people usually feel fatigued and relaxing music when people usually feel tense.

Muzak began with Major General George Owen Squier, a retired army officer born at the end of America's Civil War. He was a pioneer in military radio work, discovering in 1907 that live trees could be tapped into and used as radio antennas (tree telephony, he called it). In 1922 Squier came up with an idea he called line radio or wired wireless, in which music, news, lectures, entertainment, and advertising would be transmitted into homes through power lines . . . sort of a "cable radio" idea.

He pitched the idea to a public utility holding company in New York City called the North American Company. North American liked it and formed a subsidiary called Wired Radio, Inc. Squier always liked the brand name Kodak. So, to name his product, he wedded "music" and "Kodak," ending up with "Muzak."

Wired Radio first began broadcasting through the electrical wires of the Cleveland Illumination Company, an electric company affiliated with North American. The broadcaster took over the balcony of an electric substation and began spinning records, offering four different channels. With a low-cost receiver, people could listen to music and news by plugging into the electrical outlets that brought their power and light.

Despite a success in Cleveland, it became clear that wired radio was not going to make it in the age of wireless radio. The company took a different tack in 1934, using telephone lines instead of power lines to transmit recorded music to hotels and restaurants, providing play lists at each table so that the patrons would know what song was coming next.

The Muzak Company, hoping to expand its market, ran across research done by two British industrial psychologists about the beneficial effects of music in the workplace. The researchers issued two conclusions: First, that proper music programming was essential for increasing productivity on the job; and second, that the music must be "rationed," since music played continuously creates as much monotony as having no music at all. Based on this study, Muzak decided to begin programming music to work by, soothing yet invigorating, "rationed" in a fifteen minutes on, fifteen minutes off format. Its sales reps convinced enough business owners to try it out, and Muzak as we know it was born.

Success in New York led to a franchise system in other cities, operated under the firm rule that franchisees would play, without variation, all programs exactly as they originated from Muzak headquarters. Franchise holders have included Danny Kaye, who owned the rights to Cincinnati, and Lyndon Johnson, who owned Austin, Texas. (Because of this, he is often assumed to have been the president who first brought Muzak to the White House. Actually, it was Dwight Eisenhower.)

During World War II, the U.S. War Production Board studied the influence of Muzak on workers and decided that there was a small but measurable influence on the reduction of turnover, training, and recruitment costs, and an increase in "vigilance" on the job. Muzak began appearing in war plants around the country.

After the war, Muzak moved into thousands of banks, insurance companies, and other offices. With technological advances, Muzak began using satellite and radio channels as well as phone lines to get music to its subscribers, which now included churches, mental institutions, prisons, secret military installations, and even a whorehouse in Germany.

The songs come from all over. A repertoire manager listens to the radio to find music to re-record for the channel. Muzak prides itself on retiring schmaltzy music from the past (although if you're a Muzak-nostalgia fan, some of the older stuff can be heard in early morning hours) and keeping up with the times with "vibrant, up-to-the-moment melodies" including current Top 40 tunes. At any given time, Muzak has an active library of five thousand titles, of which about one-fifth are replaced with new titles each year.

Every song played on the channel is custom-recorded. In the 1980s, a Czech radio orchestra recorded 75 percent of their songs, but now Muzak uses a number of instrumental configurations, including synthesizers at times. But no singers—the human voice has been heard on the channel only twice in modern history: In 1981, when an announcer broke in to announce that American hostages had been released from Iran, and on Good Friday, 1985, when it joined thousands of radio stations around the world in a simultaneous broadcast of "We Are the World."

Voices are eliminated for the same reason Muzak favors violas over violins, French horns over trumpets, and a muted percussion section over drum solos—because the company doesn't want people to get distracted by the music and actually listen to it. Muzak, as the company likes to say, is to be *heard*, not *listened to*.

Each song is given a "stimulus value" score that denotes how stimulating it is, which is determined mathematically by measuring the song's tempo, rhythm, instrumentation, and size of the orchestra. Muzak arranges the songs into fifteen minute sets of five songs each, customized for each specific time of day by a computer. The music reaches peaks of liveliness at 10 A.M. and at 2 P.M., which are lull times for most workers.

Despite claims, environmental music doesn't work the same way with everybody. It is supposed to put shoppers in the mood to linger and buy, yet convenience stores in the Northwest began using it for the opposite effect: to chase away loitering teens who couldn't take another strings-and-piano rendition of "You Light Up My Life" or "Red Roses for a Blue Lady."

The company dismisses anti-Muzak critics out of hand. "You know," says a spokesperson, "pollsters have done research of the electorate, and they found that there's a certain percentage that is just anti-everything. You have a hard core that's against everything, a vocal 10 percent, and I suspect that we're hearing from that vocal fringe group many times. If a business person is considering Muzak for an office and is going to be swayed by the 10 percent that always complains about something, then he'll have a big problem running his business."

America's Biggest Defeat?
Not the *Viet* Cong . . .
Donkey Kong

What's responsible for nearly 10 percent of America's trade deficit with Japan? Our kids' obsession with Nintendo. And what started the obsession? Donkey Kong, which was Nintendo's first big hit, the first of the Super Mario series.

The Nintendo Company began over a hundred years ago in Kyoto, Japan, as a family business that manufactured playing cards. In 1889, it adopted the Nintendo name, which means, depending on context, either "Leave luck to heaven" or "Work hard, but in the end all is in heaven's hands."

After Japan's defeat in World War II, the remains of the company were taken over by twenty-year-old scion Hiroshi Yamauchi. His first big success was in the late 1950s: playing cards with Disney characters on them. Under Yamauchi's guidance, Nintendo diversified into toys. In 1960, the company had a big hit with Ultra Hand, a plastic, cross-strutted device for kids like those seen in cartoons that let characters pick up things beyond their normal reach. In 1968, Nintendo's big hit was a baseball-pitching machine.

The company moved into electronic games in the 1970s when it marketed Game & Watch, a line of inexpensive wristwatches with a primitive computer game built in. The success of the cheap games led to Nintendo's entry into arcade games.

Yamauchi noticed that video games were edging pinball out of arcades, bars, student dives, and fast-food places. His research told him that a competitor's game, Space Invaders, was attracting record numbers of coins all over the globe. He decided that he was seeing his company's future. Yamauchi assembled crews of hardware designers.

Yamauchi was personally indifferent to video games. He took perverse pride in never playing his company's games (during one video game demonstration he was handed a joystick and he threw it down in frustration, not knowing what to do with it). Regardless, Yamauchi realized that it was the software that was going to be the determining factor of his failure or success. He decided that Nintendo would become a haven for video game designers.

First of all, he forbade the marketing department from talking to them, figuring the marketers would be looking at what was currently successful, not at what would define the next trend. Unfortunately, despite his good intentions, nurturing and inspiring were not within Yamauchi's normal style—badgering and threatening were. He came up with his own method of motivating his troops: on one hand, supporting them with significant staff and resources; on the other, ruthlessly pitting his three creative teams in competition against each other. They would work for months developing games knowing that Yamauchi would pick only one of the three games for release. Although he never played video games, he believed that he was the best judge of quality. He welcomed no advice or contradiction.

His system worked well for a while. It brought forth bestselling games like the Legend of Zelda, Kid Icarus, and Metroid, an adventure game with a reverse *The Crying Game* twist (at the end, the brave warrior removes his helmet—and is revealed to be a blond-haired woman). But Nintendo's best seller of all, the one that made them what they are today, was developed when Yamauchi's harsh competitive team system laid an egg.

In 1980, Yamauchi selected a battle game called Radarscope for release to arcades. It was shipped in large numbers, including two thousand that were sent to America, in Nintendo's first major attempt to crack the market. But Yamauchi blew it this time—Radarscope was a simplistic and boring shoot-down-the-airplanes game. In arcades everywhere, Radarscope games began gathering dust.

Yamauchi got dozens of desperate calls from his sales force, including one from his son-in-law in America, who was suddenly stuck with thousands of expensive but unwanted game consoles. Yamauchi decided it was necessary to fix the game and reinstall it into the consoles that already existed in huge numbers. But who could do it? He looked around and found that all of his development teams were already over-scheduled on more important new products. In fact, the only employee who didn't seem too busy was an old friend's son he had hired three years earlier.

At that time, Sigeru Miyamoto's father had called on Yamauchi, afraid his head-in-the-clouds art student son would never get a real job on his own. Yamauchi's first reaction was "We need engineers, not painters," but he agreed to meet the boy as a favor to his friend. Miyamoto actually made a halfway decent impression on Nintendo's president and was hired as the company's first staff artist.

Yamauchi called Miyamoto to his office and told him the problem. Miyamoto replied that he always loved video games and played them in college, but could never figure out why they all were about shooting and tennis. Why weren't they created like movies or books? Why didn't they have interesting characters, plots, ideas, and myths?

Yamauchi nodded impatiently, trying to bring the conversation back to earth. Radarscope needed to be converted to something that would sell, and Miyamoto would be more or less on his own. If he fixed it, he'd be a hero. If not, well. . . .

Miyamoto returned to his desk with the schematics of Radarscope. Deciding that nothing could make the game better, he threw the schematics into his wastebasket and started daydreaming. *Beauty and the Beast* came to mind, and he started sketching his own beast, which started looking more and more like a big ape. He decided it would escape and kidnap the girlfriend of the main character and that the character would have to chase the ape through obstacles and catch him to win.

Miyamoto thought of his childhood outside Kyoto, where he would go on long adventures through fields and narrow alleys and the hallways and basements of friends. He decided to incorporate that sense of traveling through unknown pathways in the game.

Next, he started sketching the main character. Like the ape, he wanted him to be comical and unthreatening—not a superhero, but an everyday sort of guy. Miyamoto sketched him with a big nose. An engineer had told him to make characters easily identifiable on the screen, and so Miyamoto made him chubby and dressed him in a bright carpenter's outfit. He couldn't draw hairstyles very well, so he gave his character a hat. He sketched out a scenario where the carpenter would have to climb, ride, and jump up the unfinished shell of a building while trying to avoid barrels and other lethal objects thrown and rolled by the gorilla.

Needing background music and not knowing who to turn to for help, Miyamoto wrote some tunes and performed them himself on a small synthesizer. He consulted a Japanese/English dictionary and found "donkey" listed as an English equivalent to the Japanese word for stupid or goofy. He decided that Kong would be a good name for the gorilla, so he called the game Donkey Kong.

When Donkey Kong was released in Japan in 1981, the

sales force went ape. What the hell was a Donkey Kong? Games that were selling had a shooting and killing theme and a name to match. At least one rep resigned in protest and despair.

In America, the reaction was similar. Yamauchi's son-in-law, Minoru Arakawa, received a prototype board and anxiously adapted one of the Radarscope games. When he plugged it in, his heart sank when the name came up on the screen. He decided that this was going to sell even worse than Radarscope did. When he started playing, it seemed to confirm his worst fears—a disaster! He called his father-in-law and asked him to at least change the name. Yamauchi refused. "It's a good game," he said.

Arakawa knew he had no choice than to try and sell it. He went back to his workshop, where he found one of his young staff playing it intently. In fact, they nearly had to pry the kid away from the game. Hmm, maybe there's hope, thought Arakawa.

Before production could begin, the Americans had to provide English text to replace the Japanese in the original. They started to name the characters. The princess was named after a sales manager's wife. They were trying to decide what to call the carpenter when there was a knock at the door. It was the owner of the warehouse, who had come to loudly complain that he hadn't received that month's rent. Arakawa promised that he'd get the money the next day, and the man stomped out. His name was Mario Segali. "Mario!" somebody shouted. "Super Mario!" That was the name they settled on for the character.

Within days, it was clear they had a winner. The machines attracted quarters like magnets, and Arakawa's phone started ringing endlessly. Nintendo of America made $100 million that year, most of which came directly from Donkey Kong.

Over the next ten years, Miyamoto designed eight more Super Mario games for arcade and home use. The character changed a little. He became a plumber instead of a carpenter, and he obtained a brother. The games sold about 70 million copies, surviving imitators, plagiarists, skeleton turtles, and, scariest of all, entertainment conglomerate MCA, which sued unsuccessfully over the gorilla named Kong.

Not all video game success stories have ended happily for their originators. At another company, Namco, a video game called PacMan sold millions of units and made the company rich. The grateful and newly affluent president, sitting on hundreds of millions of dollars of sales and spinoffs, called the game's designer into his office and presented him with a bonus for his successful effort. The check was for a paltry $3,500. The designer went to his office, cleaned out his desk, and vowed never to design another video game as long as he lived.

But it was different with Donkey Kong. Miyamoto was again summoned to Yamauchi's office, who explained that he needed new and imaginative games, especially for the home game modules that were being rolled out. He told the former art student he was making him head of Nintendo's new entertainment division. Over the following decade and beyond, Miyamoto supervised Nintendo's most imaginative games.

Biting the Wax Tadpole of International Marketing

Cracking an international market is a goal of most growing corporations. It shouldn't be that hard. Yet even the big multinationals run into trouble because of language and cultural differences:

• The name Coca-Cola in China was first rendered as Ke-kou-ke-la. Unfortunately, the Coke company didn't discover until after thousands of signs had been printed that the phrase means "bite the wax tadpole" or "female horse stuffed with wax." Coke researched 40,000 Chinese characters and found a close phonetic equivalent, "ko-kou-ko-le," which can be loosely translated as "happiness in the mouth."

• In Taiwan, the translation of Pepsi's slogan "Come alive with the Pepsi Generation" came out "Pepsi will bring your ancestors back from the dead."

• Also in Chinese, the Kentucky Fried Chicken slogan "finger-lickin' good" came out as "eat your fingers off."

• The American slogan for Salem cigarettes, "Salem—Feeling Free," got translated for the Japanese market into "When smoking Salem, you feel so refreshed that your mind seems to be clear and empty."

• When General Motors introduced the Chevy Nova in South America, it was apparently unaware that "*no va*" means "it won't go." After the company figured out why it wasn't selling any cars, it renamed the car, in Spanish markets, the Caribe.

• Ford had a similar problem in Brazil when the Pinto flopped. The company found out that Pinto was Brazilian slang for tiny male genitals. Ford pried the nameplates off and substituted Corcel, which means horse.

• When the Parker Pen Company marketed a ballpoint pen in Mexico, its ads were *supposed* to say "It won't leak in your pocket and embarrass you." However, the company's translators mistakenly thought the spanish word "embarazar" meant "embarrass"—it doesn't. So the ad promised, "It won't leak in your pocket and make you pregnant."

• Even the U.S. Spanish-speaking market can be tough. An Anglo T-shirt maker in Miami *thought* he was printing a souvenir shirt during the Pontiff's visit that said "I saw the Pope" in Spanish. Instead, the shirts translated to "I saw the Potato."

• Frank Purdue's slogan, "It takes a tough man to make a tender chicken," got mangled in a similarly bad Spanish translation. A photo of Purdue with one of his birds appeared on billboards all over Mexico, captioned "It takes a hard man to make a chicken aroused."

• Hunt-Wesson introduced its Big John products in French Canada as Gros Jos before finding out that the phrase was slang for "big breasts." In this case, though, the bad translation didn't seem to hurt sales.

• Colgate, already in trouble for its Darkie toothpaste in Asia (complete with big-lipped minstrel logo), stepped into it again when it introduced a toothpaste in France called Cue, which is the name of a notorious pornographic magazine.

• In Italy, an advertising campaign for Schweppes Tonic Water translated the name into Schweppes Toilet Water.

JACK MINGO

• Japan's second-largest tourist agency was mystified when it entered English-speaking markets. It kept attracting travelers who wanted unusual sex tours. When they found out why, the owners of Kinki Nippon Tourist Company changed its name.

Johnson & Johnson's Band-Aid Solution

Johnson & Johnson should actually be called Johnson & Johnson & Johnson. It was actually three brothers, Robert, James, and Edward, who founded the company in 1885. Nine years earlier, Robert had heard English surgeon Joseph Lister speak on his theory of airborne germs as a source of infection in the operating room (he called them the "invisible assassins").

In the 1800s, most surgeons held Lister's theory in contempt. How could they be contaminating their own patients by operating ungloved with unsterile instruments? Amazingly, surgeons normally operated in street clothes under rarely washed blood-spattered lab coats—and then dressed the patient's surgical wounds with cotton scraps swept up from the floors of textile mills. Doctors apparently thought it was just coincidence that the postoperative mortality rate in some hospitals ran as high as 90 percent.

Robert Johnson concluded that Lister was right and decided there would soon be a market for antiseptic surgical dressing. He joined with his brothers in New Brunswick, New Jersey, and began manufacturing ready-made cotton and gauze dressing sealed in individual packages, using dry heat and an aseptic environment to produce a sterile product.

In 1899, Johnson & Johnson introduced a surgical tape with zinc oxide adhesive that was designed to hold the dressing to skin without irritating it. Through the next few decades, the company concentrated on operating room supplies, including things like a catgut sterilizer for ensuring aseptic sutures. But, in the early 1920s, it was ready to diversify into the consumer market.

Luckily, Josephine Dickson was something of a klutz. She was the new bride of Johnson & Johnson cotton buyer Earle Dickson, and she was just getting the hang of the wifely duty of housework. Cooking was the worst. She regularly cut herself with sharp knives or burned herself on the handles of pots and pans.

A more enlightened husband of the Roaring Twenties might have taken her to a disciple of Freud to find out why she felt the need to punish herself. Earle, however, patiently bandaged her hands with the dressing and surgical tape he took home as a perk of employment, using a bedside technique that he learned from his father and grandfather, both of whom were doctors. However, the process was clumsy, requiring two free hands, and he wasn't always home. Not wanting his wife to be forced into depending on the kindness of neighbors (or worse, the iceman), Earle sat in deep thought "determined," as he put it later, "to devise some manner of bandage that would stay in place, be easily applied, and still retain its sterility."

He laid out a three-inch-wide strip of surgical tape on his kitchen table, sticky side up. He rolled up a pad of gauze and stuck it across the middle of the tape. To keep the pad clean and the adhesive from drying out, he covered it all with a piece of crinoline cloth. The idea was that when Mrs. Dickson injured herself again, she could slice off a piece of the Earl's tape-and-bandage, remove the crinoline, and apply her own dressing with her one good hand.

Dickson mentioned his invention to a fellow employee, who encouraged him to tell his story to management. Johnson & Johnson president James Johnson saw the potential of the product, and the superintendent of J&J's cotton mill, W. Johnson

Kenyon, came up with the name: "band" for the tape strip, and "aid," as in first-aid.

The first Band-Aids were made by hand and produced in sections three inches wide by eighteen inches long. Like poor Mrs. Dickson, the user was expected to slice off a piece as needed. Sales were slow at first, so the company began pushing them heavily through its house-generated magazines for druggists and doctors (these were edited by Dr. Frederick B. Kilmer, the father of poet Joyce "Only God Can Make a Tree" Kilmer).

The company started giving out free samples. The Boy Scouts got a bunch. So did every butcher in Cleveland. In 1924, Johnson & Johnson came up with a machine to precut the bandages into three inch by three-quarter inch slices. The added convenience increased sales 50 percent in one year. Physicians began using them for protecting small cuts and covering smallpox vaccinations. Circus workers found them ideal for covering scratches from tent stakes and rope burns.

Did Mrs. Dickson get adept at cooking and stop hurting herself? Company archives are silent on that matter. But we do know that Earle Dickson jumped onto the fast track at Johnson & Johnson, becoming a member of the board of directors in 1929 and a vice president in 1932. He died in 1962.

How Greyhound Put
on the Dog

"Leave the driving to us." Greyhound, the oldest and most well-known bus company in America, began as a one-Hupmobile line in Hibbing, Minnesota (later the birthplace of Bob Dylan, who—unlike Paul Simon and Johnny Mercer—never once wrote a song about Greyhound buses).

Hibbing, seventy-five miles northwest of Duluth, was incorporated as a village in 1893, but, a few years later, a huge deposit of iron ore was discovered under its streets. The entire village was picked up and moved two miles to the south to make way for an open pit mine called the Mahoning.

In 1913, two enterprising Swedish émigrés named Carl Wickman and Andrew Anderson got tired of working as drillers for the mine. They decided to pool their savings and start a Hupmobile dealership, selling seven-passenger touring cars designed by Bobby Hupp, who was once the right-hand man of Ransom E. Olds, founder of Oldsmobile.

Unfortunately, the partners didn't have much money, and they weren't very good salesmen. Nobody in Hibbing came in to buy the single Hupmobile they had in their stock.

Most of the residents of Hibbing were miners who worked the Mahoning mine. They couldn't afford to buy a car; in fact, most couldn't afford transportation to work, so they commuted four miles by foot every day. Some miners lived in a settlement named Alice, two miles south of Hibbing. Their round-trip was eight miles.

Watching their former coworkers trudging past their car dealership gave the two Swedes an idea. Wickman and Anderson decided to forget about selling their Hupmobile. Instead, they sold rides in it.

On the first trip they collected $2.25. While not a fortune, it encouraged them to continue. They began an hourly run from the fire hall in Alice to a saloon in Hibbing to the mines and then back again. They tried charging an outrageous $1.50 for the round-trip, but quickly dropped the fare to 15¢ one way, 25¢ both ways, when they figured out that they could squeeze as many as eighteen passengers into the seven-person car by stacking them up inside and using the running boards and bumpers.

Formally the Hibbing Transportation Company, the one-Hup line was popularly known as the Snoose Line ("snoose" being the Swedish word for chewing tobacco—the miners were heavy users, and passengers had to be constantly on guard for wind-borne expectorations). The Snoose grew popular enough that they customized the Hupmobile to hold more passengers. They then recruited another Swede, Arvid Heed, into their partnership because he owned his own Buick. With two cars and three drivers, the Snoose Line became an around-the-clock service.

In 1915, they bought two buses mounted on truck chassis and expanded their service area to include the little town of Nashwauk, fifteen miles north. Meanwhile, though, competition reared its ugly head. Ralph Bogan started covering the same route with his Studebaker, charging a little less for the trip. A price war developed—until both sides realized that they were losing money. The Snoose Line did for the first time what Greyhound later made into an art form—they offered Bogan a partnership if he would join their company.

The partners expanded their line to Duluth and changed its name to the Mesaba Transportation Company. In 1926, Wickman sold his share of the company for $60,000 and started a holding company, the Motor Transit Corporation, with financing by the Great Northern Railroad. MTC began buying up little bus companies around the Great Lakes area. One of them was the Safety Motor Coach Lines, run by E. C. Eckstrom, who, as part of the deal, became president of the MTC. Eckstrom's buses at that time were popularly called "greyhounds," but how they got that name is not clear. There are at least two different stories:

1. Eckstrom had his buses painted battleship gray to hide the grime of the road. An innkeeper joked to him one day that the buses "looked just like greyhounds streaking by" and the name stuck.

2. The Fageol Brothers in Oakland, California, made buses by stretching passenger cars and doubling their seating capacity. They painted the over-long vehicles gray. Drivers nicknamed them "dachshunds," but a driver in California, disliked the name and claimed that his bus was faster than that—it was really a "greyhound."

Regardless, Wickman liked the Greyhound name. In 1926, he decided to have Eckstrom's running-dog insignia painted on all of MTC's buses. Within a decade that was an awful lot of buses—the Big Dog ate up dozens of lesser dogs of the bus business, creating a network that spanned the country from coast to coast.

Ironically, the Greyhound Company got out of the bus business in 1987, creating no end of confusion. Like many corporate giants in the last few decades, Greyhound decided to diversify into a conglomerate of unrelated businesses, buying up Armour Meat, Dial Soap, and Dobbs airport concessions, while selling off its bus line to a group of Texas investors. Logically, the new bus company called itself Greyhound Lines, Inc.

Illogically, the now busless conglomerate retained the Greyhound name as well, becoming the Greyhound-Dial Corporation in 1990.

More recently, the company has accepted reality and dropped the Greyhound misnomer. It now calls itself simply the Dial Corporation.

How a Cute Mascot Can Reform the Image of a Sullied Corporation

With the exception of the Energizer bunny, the Snuggles bear, and a handful of others, the heyday of mythical corporate symbols seems to have passed. The public may love Mr. Whipple and Betty Crocker and (especially) the cute spokesanimal cartoon characters like Tony the Tiger and Charlie Tuna, but most advertising agencies hate them because there's no challenge to them. Not only that, but, if they're successful, they lock the client into variations of the same kind of advertising for years into the future, making it hard to justify big, continuing "creative" costs.

Still, the use of "cute" has been especially successful with companies that realize that they are perceived as big, greedy, impersonal, and heartless. Metropolitan Life, for example, effectively softened its image as another one of those money-sucking insurance companies by hiring Snoopy as its sales rep.

This is a fine and proud tradition in the corporate world. It's surprising more greedy and impersonal companies don't use it. Could Exxon have softened the bad publicity about its Alaskan oil spill if it had come out with some cartoon entity like Edgar, the Exxon Ecology Egret? Could the savings and loan industry have saved itself from disgrace if it had been represented in the public eye by Linus the Credit Lion? If Elsie the Cow and Chiquita Banana are any indication, it just might have worked.

HOW ELSIE BECAME BORDEN'S CASH COW

Before Gail Borden discovered how to condense whole milk in the 1850s, he was the official state surveyor for the state of Texas (among other things, he laid out the streets of Galveston) and founder of the weekly *Telegraph and Texas Register*. He was also a tinkerer and inventor. He designed a portable bathhouse for women to change in on the beach, a steamboat to be driven by mechanical oars, a lazy Susan for quick table service, a vehicle he called the "terraqueus" because it could travel on both land and water, and even a "simplified method" to make it easy to convert Catholics into Protestants. But none of these amounted to anything.

Borden had long been interested in condensing and preserving food. He poured his heart, soul, and finances into one he called the meat biscuit. He'd take 120 pounds of beef and boil it down to ten pounds of beef jelly, which he mixed with flour and baked into long-lasting biscuits for travelers. His biscuits won awards at exhibitions, including the prestigious London International Exhibition in 1851. They were even taken along by a group of forty-niners on their way to California. There was only one problem: They tasted absolutely foul. They were even too bad for the army's notoriously low aesthetic standards—after field tests, a board of army officers reported that Borden's biscuits were "not only unpalatable," but that they produced "headache and nausea."

On the ship home from London after winning his award, Borden was confronted with the sight of distraught immigrant mothers holding crying, dying babies in the steerage compartment because the two cows aboard the steamer were giving infected milk. Borden is said to have been "haunted" by what he saw and decided to find a way to preserve milk for long periods of time.

Meanwhile, however, his meat biscuit empire was crumbling around him. Now a penniless widower, he sent his four children off to live with the Shaker religious colony in Lebanon, New York, and began living and working in a cellar in Brooklyn. He tried boiling gallons of milk down to quarts, but the dark substance that remained tasted horrible, like burnt molasses.

He had a stroke of luck when he visited his children at the Shaker colony. The Shakers were well known for their inventive and functional designs. Borden noticed some of them making fruit preserves with a device of their own invention: a "vacuum pan" from which most of the air had been pumped out. It worked on the principle that liquids in a near-vacuum boil at a lower temperature. Borden made his own vacuum pan and found that milk would boil at 136° F. instead of 212° leaving its color and taste essentially unchanged. He discovered he could remove 80 percent of the water from milk, leaving a heavy fluid that, when preserved with sugar, could last indefinitely and didn't taste too bad.

Financial success, however, eluded him. Marketing the viscous liquid as milk was not as easy as he had hoped at first. He had to sell half his company to keep it going. Luckily, about that time, a muckraking editor of *Leslie's Illustrated Weekly* launched a lurid exposé of "swill milk" with vivid word pictures of urban milk supplies from diseased cows fed on brewery refuse, milk cans and manure being hauled on the same carts, and "milk murder!"—high infant death rates from typhoid and tuberculosis. Capitalizing on the uproar, Borden bought ads extolling the purity of his condensed "country milk." Sales picked up.

In fact, the Borden Company thrived so much in following decades that in the 1930s it became the subject of controversy. People began wondering why, if milk cost so much, the dairy farmers were paid so little. In the ensuing "milk wars," the big milk wholesalers, distributors, and retailers were blamed for jacking up prices and pocketing obscene profits. The Borden Company, now one of the biggest middlemen, decided it needed to quickly change its public image from rapacious and greedy . . . to cute and cuddly.

Company executives decided to milk their obvious assets and came up with cartoon spokescows in humorous comic strips. They tried them in medical journals first, with such laugh-riot hijinx as:

CALF: "Mama, I think I see a germ!"
COW: "Mercy, child—run quick for the Borden Inspector!"

Doctors swamped the company with requests for reprints for their waiting room walls, so Borden began running the ads in New York newspapers. There was a herd of cartoon cows with names like Bessie, Clara, Mrs. Blossom, and Elsie. Then, in 1938, a radio copywriter randomly singled out Elsie's name in a commercial for Rush Hughes, a network news commentator who was sponsored by Borden. Hughes read aloud a letter, purportedly from a cow to her mother:

Dear Mama:
    I'm so excited I can hardly chew. We girls are sending our milk to Borden now!

Love, Elsie

The commercial so tickled Hughes's listeners that they started sending fan mail to Elsie. She quickly became Borden's one sacred cow, and made her debut in national magazines like *Life* and the *Saturday Evening Post*. For the New York World's Fair, the company bought a seven-year-old, 950-pound Jersey from Brookfield, Massachusetts, whose registered name was "You'll Do, Lobelia," and called her Elsie. They set her up in an exhibit that was supposedly her bedroom. It was done up in "Barn Colonial" with churns used as tables, milk bottles as lamps, a wheelbarrow for a chaise longue, and oil paintings of Elsie's ancestors. She was such a media hit that she was asked to costar in the movie *Little Men* with Jack Oakie and Kay Francis in 1940.

About the same time, the cartoon cow became married to Elmer and had two calves, Beulah and Beauregard (named after the Confederate General in the Battle of Bull Run). The family ruled the barnyard for nearly three decades. The company even named a glue after Elmer. They didn't use Elsie's name because they feared that consumers would think the glue was made from over-the-hill dairy cows.

In 1969, Borden's chairman, caught up in the diversification fever of the time, decided that Elsie gave "an inaccurate message" about the company, forgetting that that had been the whole point in the first place. He decided that a company bent on diversifying into chemical manufacturing should downplay an animal that had long been meant to symbolize wholesome country goodness. Elsie was dropped as a corporate symbol, even though polls indicated she was among the best-known corporate mascots, in favor of an abstract red oval. Among themselves employees derided the abstract oval as "the toilet seat." Eventually a new management team took over, which recognized the value of Elsie's recognition among consumers. On March 10, 1993, Borden readopted her to represent all of its dairy brands, building a new logo around her smiling cow face.

HOW CHIQUITA BANANA GOT UNITED FRUIT OFF ON A PEEL

*I'm Chiquita Banana and I've come to say
Bananas have to ripen in a certain way . . .*

Chiquita Banana, the wacky singing Latin American banana, was the response that the United Fruit Company came up with to counteract their negative image.

In the court of world public opinion, the United Fruit Company was guilty as charged. The company had a well-deserved reputation of ruthlessness among our good neighbors down in South America. It bought up millions of acres of land (sometimes merely to keep it out of the hands of competitors) . . . and as many government officials as it could. The governments it couldn't buy, it worked to overthrow. Often, as in places like Guatemala in 1954, it received the support of the United States government. In fact, the term "banana republic" was originally coined as a backhanded tribute to United Fruit's ability to enforce whatever corrupt government it wanted, by ballot or bullet.

The company had so much cheap land that it didn't bother with maintaining the soil—when a plantation was exhausted, the company abandoned it. They'd load everything of value onto rail cars, tearing up the railroad tracks after them, and bulldoze another plantation out of the rain forest. It was costly to the land and the company, but absolutely disastrous for its workers, who were abandoned along with the used-up plantations.

All of these practices engendered a lot of hard feelings and unfavorable publicity for the company. In Cuba, United Fruit lost all its holdings when two sons of a lifelong United Fruit employee, Angel Castro, led a successful revolution against the banana-corrupted government. (Years later, company executives who knew Angel couldn't help but shake their heads and wonder aloud how a couple of quiet and polite kids like Fidel and Raul Castro could have gone so wrong.) It was a revolution that even United Fruit couldn't undo. Not that it didn't try—the company secretly provided two freighters from its Great White Fleet to transport fighters and weapons into Cuba during the ill-fated Bay of Pigs invasion.

But that was later. Lovable Miss Chiquita Banana was born two decades before Castro's revolution, as World War II began winding down. The Great White Fleet had been repainted battleship gray and pressed into emergency service by the navy. The numbers of bananas coming into the United States turned into a trickle. United Fruit's corporate leaders had kept their plantations going even though they didn't have a way to get the bananas to market. Now they began planning a postwar blitz. As soon as they could, they once again began shipping a hundred million bunches of bananas a year.

Most Americans hadn't seen a banana since shortly after the attack on Pearl Harbor, three years earlier. The company directors decided this was a splendid opportunity to carve out a brand new cute and cuddly image for the company.

They turned the problem over to their radio ad agency, Batten, Barton, Durstine & Osborn, which came up with a wacky but sexy female Latin American singer modeled after Carmen Miranda, even choosing a name that aped hers and stealing her trademark, a fruit-covered hat. The agency assigned two staff jingle writers, lyricist Garth Montgomery and songsmith Len MacKenzie, to write the song.

United Fruit pushed the song into the public's consciousness by insisting that the song be played by all the musicians who played on radio shows it sponsored. Radio listeners heard the song rendered by such varied performers as Fred Allen, Alec Templeton, Arthur Fiedler, Bert Lahr, the King Sisters, Xavier Cugat, Charlie McCarthy, Carmen Miranda herself, and even fictional detective Ellery Queen ("I'm Chiquita Banana and I'm here to say / You have to catch a criminal in a certain way / Now here's the strategy I've tried to use: I have paid real strict attention to all of the clues. . . ."). At its peak, the song was played around the country on radio 276 times in one day. Recorded on disk by Ray Bloch and the King Sisters, it started showing up on jukeboxes as well.

Chiquita Banana was a genuine hit, and the public began clamoring to see what she looked like. The company commissioned comic artist Dik Browne, who had just finished redesigning the Campbell Kids, but had yet to create the comic strip Hägar the Horrible. He drew Chiquita as a banana with a ruffled skirt, puffy sleeves, and a fruit covered wide-brimmed hat. She began appearing in magazine ads and finally in eighty-second cartoon shorts where she sang to movie audiences in 850 movie theaters across the country.

At first United Fruit was happy, even delirious, about the success of Chiquita and her song. But over time they began getting uneasy. True, Chiquita sold the idea of banana consumption, which helped them—but she also helped their competitors, because consumers couldn't differentiate United Fruit bananas from the others in the store.

Jack Fox, an executive vice president who had been hired away from Coca-Cola, called a meeting one day to complain that Chiquita was a brand name of United Fruit and all the other banana companies were getting a free ride. He announced that, somehow, they were going to start branding their bananas within six to eight weeks.

The old-timers scoffed—the company had been trying to figure out how to brand bananas for years, and now this new soft drink guy was going to do it in six weeks? Fox continued that he didn't know what form the branding would take—maybe a rubber stamp or electrostatic printing (like a Xerox machine, where a machine imprints a negative charge that attracts ink particles) or maybe a gummed sticker attached to every third banana.

"Stickers?" snorted one Southern old-timer who felt secure enough in his job to challenge the vice president. "Shee-it! Do you realize how many that would be in a year? *One billion* stickers. You've got to be out of your mind!"

Fox, clearly taken aback by the number, asked him to repeat the number of labels he had calculated.

"One billion!"

The room erupted in nervous laughter. Fox looked at him steadily and the laughter stopped. Fox nodded his head. "That's just what I make it. One billion."

Stickers seemed like the best way to go, even though further calculations made it clear that the company would actually need 2½ billion stickers that year. When they contacted their sticker vendor with the order, his eyes rolled back, and he quietly fell backward in a faint.

The company designed labels with the Chiquita name and drawing prominently displayed against a field of light blue. But finding a way to apply the labels inexpensively was the biggest problem. United Fruit called in machinery experts from around the country, but none of their solutions were simple and cheap enough (their consensus was that the cost of the machinery, operator, and the labels would come out to about ten dollars per labeled banana). The solution came from an unexpected source: A young worker in a Honduras plantation came up with a simple device that had no moving parts and was powered by a squeeze of the operator's hand.

United Fruit quickly became the largest single buyer of

pressure-sensitive labels in the world, using more than three billion a year. The commercials and stickers had such an impact that the Chiquita name became much more famous than that of United Fruit. The company further muddied its image by changing its name to United Brands in the 1960s. It finally got smart and changed its name to Chiquita Brands International in 1990 and began using the smiling banana lady as its corporate symbol.

How a Man Who Would Be King Gave America Its Closest Shave

King Camp Gillette came by his eccentricity honestly. First of all, there was his name, given in honor of his father's friend, Judge King (Judge was his given name, not his title—just as King Gillette wasn't really a king, Judge wasn't really a judge).

Then there was his mom, Fanny Lemira Camp, who took lifelong pride in having been the first white woman born in Ann Arbor, Michigan. She was author of *The White House Cookbook*, available in various editions for a century since its debut in 1887; for most of King's childhood, his mom served up experimental recipes like Georgia Possum Pie or Rattlesnake Filet and took post-dinner polls on whether to include them in her cookbook.

Gillette's father, George, was a postmaster and part-time inventor whose hardware-supply business had been wiped out by the Chicago Fire in 1871. In 1872, when King was seventeen, he followed in his father's footsteps. He got himself hired by a hardware supply business. Four years later, he was promoted from clerk to traveling sales rep.

While on the road, King filled his spare time by inventing things. In 1879, he patented a combination bushing and valve for faucets. Ten years later he patented two new types of electrical conduits. None of his inventions made him any significant money, but he continued his tinkering.

One of his bosses appreciated Gillette's salesmanship and understood his drive to invent. He was William Painter, president of the Baltimore Seal Company, himself a successful inventor. One of Painter's money-making inventions was a soft-rubber valve used in emptying cesspools and privy pits. But the one that made him rich beyond dreams was the Crown Cork, the cork-lined metal bottle cap still in use today.

Painter adopted the forty-year-old Gillette as a protégé and personal friend and in 1885 gave Gillette a piece of advice that inspired him for years afterward: "King, why don't you try to come up with something like the Crown Cork, which, when used, is thrown away? The customer keeps coming back for more; with each additional customer you get, you are building a foundation of profit."

"That sounds simple enough," replied King, "but how many things are there like corks, pins, and needles?"

Painter paused, thoughtfully. "You don't know. It isn't probable that you will ever find anything that is like the Crown Cork, but it won't do any harm to think about it." King did, to a point of obsession. He kept his mind constantly busy, watching life around him and waiting for inspiration to hit. He went through the dictionary, compiling page after page of things people needed, but for the longest time, he couldn't think of anything that people would want to use once and then throw away.

That's when a different kind of revelation hit. It had nothing to do with inventing things. It was bigger than that, much bigger. Gillette's revelation had to do with reinventing humanity's place in the entire social and economic system.

It came to him in a hotel room in Scranton, Pennsylvania. A heavy storm was raging and the rain fell in torrents. Normally dependable to a fault, Gillette decided to cancel his appointments for the day. He sat in his room, looking out at the rain-snarled traffic below his window. In the wind and rain, a disorganized mess of horses, buggies, and pedestrians had achieved a pre-auto state of gridlock.

First, Gillette tried to figure out ways that the snarl could
have been avoided; then his mind was blown far adrift. Looking down on the disabled grocery wagon that had caused the
snarl, he began imagining what was inside and where it came
from, tracing coffee back through grinding and roasting to
plantations in Brazil; following sugar back to the cane fields of
Cuba; and chasing spices back to the Orient.

Until that point, he wrote later, he had always thought of the
world's industries as separate, independent entities. But suddenly
"came the thought that is destined to change man's conception
of industry. The thought—*Industry as a whole is one vast operative
mechanism. Included in it are the governments of every country, and
our combined system of social, political and industrial economy.*" He
began seeing the whole world as one giant machine. But that
machine was running inefficiently and needed someone who
could put it back in order through "the displacement of governments and the amalgamation of all the people in the world into
one corporate body, with one corporate brain."

Gillette decided that he was that someone. He decided to
write a book: a practical, step-by-step guide to centralize the
entire world into one gigantic corporation. He put aside the
idea of inventing gadgets and began reinventing the world.

In the summer of 1894, he finished his book and got it
published under the name *The Human Drift.* He sat back and
waited for the world to see the rightness of his cause and began
readying himself to take over as head of the worldwide Twentieth Century Company. His book began getting glowing
reviews in utopian and socialist publications. Letters of support
started filling his mailbox, some of them containing money to
buy shares in Twentieth Century.

But, as he waited to become the world's chairman of the
board, the next revelation struck, the one that would sidetrack
him from his world-saving goals.

It happened while doing his morning ablutions in a hotel room. Gillette wrote, years later, that

> on one particular morning when I started to shave, I found my razor dull, and it was not only dull, but was beyond the point of successful stropping and it needed honing, for which it must be taken to a barber or a cutler. As I stood there with the razor in my hand, my eyes resting on it lightly as a bird settling down on its nest . . . the thought occurred to me that no radical improvements had been made in razors, especially in razor blades, for several centuries, and it flashed through my mind that if by any possibility razor blades could be constructed and made cheap enough to do away with honing and stropping and permit the user to replace dull blades by new ones, such improvements would be highly important in that art. . . . The Gillette razor was born.

Well, not quite. It took another eight years for Gillette to work out the practical details, assisted by an engineer named William E. Nickerson. (Can you imagine the marketing difficulties if the razor had been named after him?) Expert cutlers and metallurgists said that it couldn't be done, but Gillette continued trying new metals and various designs for the handles. He finally worked out all the bugs and made the razor available to the public in 1903.

His company sold only 51 razors and 168 blades that year. Gillette continued to earn his living as a traveling salesman for Crown Cork and Seal. In September 1903, he was assigned to a selling route in England, giving him a raise he couldn't afford to turn down. He went across the sea, reluctantly leaving the Gillette Razor Company in the hands of its board of directors.

While he was gone, the company seemed about to go under and the board briefly considered selling its assets and

going out of business. But suddenly sales figures began to climb, helped along by good word-of-mouth and an extremely modest level of advertising. The company sold 91,000 razors and 123,000 blades in 1904. In November of that year, Gillette resigned his sales position and returned home.

But he was still interested in utopian politics. He wrote more books. He put his name and picture on each package of blades to increase his fame, still hoping to be made leader of the world by public acclaim. Later, when it became clear that the world was not buying his leadership role, he offered former president Teddy Roosevelt $1 million to serve as the head of the World Corporation. But Teddy declined, and when Gillette died in 1931, the world revolution he dreamed about still had not come about. To Gillette's profound disappointment, he didn't become renowned for having saved mankind; instead, he became famous for having *shaved* it.

How Unclean Dippers Got America Whistling Dixie

Billions of paper cups litter the landscape every year, both figuratively and literally. They're used in homes, schools, offices, and fast food restaurants all around the world. But did you know that paper cups were an accidental by-product of a long-ago public health campaign?

In 1907, Kansas-born Hugh Moore left the family farm and traveled east to seek his fortune. He ended up in Boston and enrolled in Harvard. His brother-in-law, Lawrence Luellen, had spent years inventing a coin-operated, water-dispensing machine. He convinced Moore to drop out of college to help get the business going.

The machine needed disposable cups, so Luellen folded and glued some out of writing paper. The partners placed their white porcelain vending machines in railroad stations and on city streets, offering seven ounces of water in a paper cup for one cent. But sales were slow because most towns had free public water troughs with tin dippers attached from which anybody could get a free drink. Why would anybody pay for something they could get free?

The machine got a small boost when the Anti-Saloon League endorsed it, reasoning that many men who wanted nothing more than a good and healthy drink wandered into saloons and were corrupted there. It got a larger boost when a young public health officer from Dodge City, Kansas, declared war on public drinking places and unsanitary communal tin dippers. Dr. Samuel Crumbine told anybody who would listen lurid but accurate accounts of the diseases, like tuberculosis, that could be contracted from public dippers. He successfully lobbied the state of Kansas to outlaw dippers in public places, including on passenger trains passing through the state.

Despite this boost, it became clear that the water vending machine was doomed. Nobody was buying water. While thinking about the situation one day, it suddenly occurred to Moore that they were selling the wrong product: Rather than selling water in a free paper cup, they should forget the water and sell the cup. He figured that public consciousness about unsanitary drinking facilities would create a big demand for disposable cups in all sorts of places. In 1910, the partners moved the company to New York, changed its name to the Individual Drinking Cup Company, dubbed the new product Health Kups, and began seeking outside financing for high speed cup-making machinery.

After being turned down by dozens of bankers and business people, Moore and Luellen approached W. T. Graham, the president of the American Can Company. Graham was, depending on which account you read, either advanced in his thinking about public hygiene or extremely phobic about germs and contamination. Either way, after hearing Moore and Luellen's lurid pitch about disease and death lurking on every public drinking glass, he agreed to put up $200,000.

Moore, using his home-state connections, traveled to Kansas and convinced Crumbine to publicly recommend disposable paper cups as the only reasonable answer to the dipper sanitation problem. Soon after, a Lafayette College professor published a study showing the wide variety of viral germs he had collected from public drinking glasses in schools. A wave of panicky concern rose up among parents, school administrators, and health workers.

Moore shamelessly fanned the flames with ads and promotional material. One was headlined "Spare the Children" and showed a clearly diseased man in what looked like the final stages of tuberculosis drinking from a dipper—while an innocent young girl waited her turn. "Avoid the common drinking cup as if it were the plague itself. In offices, theaters, stores, on trains—wherever you find it, shun it," admonished another advertisement. "The dark cloud of an influenza epidemic again threatens. . . . Influenza sits on the brim of the common drinking cup."

Health Kups caught on. By 1912, state after state followed Kansas's example. The tin dipper disappeared and paper cup dispensers appeared in schools, offices, and trains. Meanwhile, though, Moore was becoming disenchanted with the name Health Kups, figuring that it sounded too clinical. Next door to the Health Kups factory was the Dixie Doll Company. Moore had become good friends with the owner and, liking the look and sound of the word "dixie," he asked the doll manufacturer if he could borrow the name. His friend had no objections, and over next few years the friendlier-sounding Dixie Cups moved into home kitchens and bathrooms as well as into the ice cream and soft drink cup trade.

Damn that Ralph Nader!

Hell, there's more nitrates in a kiss than in a ton of bacon.
—Larry Lee, National Pork Producers' Council

If no changes are made, either by Congress or the EPA, we will not be able to build cars after late 1974 because we will not be able to meet the standards.
—Henry Ford II, whining about clean air mandates

All this concern about auto safety . . . it's of the same order as the hula hoop—a fad. Six months from now, we'll probably be on another kick.
—W. B. Murphy, president, Campbell's Soup Company commenting, for some reason, on auto issues

I find it difficult to believe that the seat belt can afford the driver any great amount of protection over and above that which is available to him through the medium of the safety-type steering wheel if he has his hands on the wheel and grips the rim sufficiently tight to take advantage of its energy absorption properties and also takes advantage of the shock-absorbing action which can be achieved by correct positioning of the feet and legs.
—Howard Gandelot, vehicle safety engineer for General Motors, 1954

. . . AND DAMN LADY BIRD JOHNSON, TOO!

We should not fall prey to the beautification extremists who have no sense of economic reality.
                    —Fred L. Hartley, president, Union Oil

Uninterrupted scenery, too, can get pretty monotonous. Billboards are only a way of humanizing what is still an overwhelming landscape.
                    —June Martino, McDonald's executive, 1959

How Lloyd's of London Got Out of Coffee . . . and into Hot Water

Lloyd's of London is the most famous insurance syndicate in history. Its underwriters' willingness to take on unusual insurance policies on things like Betty Grable's legs and Bruce Springsteen's voice have made it a risk taker's haven and a press agent's dream. In recent years, it has been in the news because a series of unlucky disasters, including the Exxon *Valdez* oil spill, Hurricane Hugo, and two big earthquakes in California, pushed many of its investors and underwriters to the edge of bankruptcy.

If Lloyd's doesn't survive as an insurance provider, maybe it can go back to the business where it began three centuries ago, as a coffeehouse.

London was the maritime center in the seventeenth century, with merchant ships coming and going constantly from its bustling harbor. At the same time, coffee-drinking was becoming popular across Europe since Dutch colonists had recently established coffee plantations on the island of Java. In 1689, the year that William and Mary took the throne of England, Edward Lloyd opened a coffeehouse on Tower Street near the docks.

Unlike taverns, where drunken revelry reigned, coffeehouses were sober places where business people went to do serious wheeling and dealing. Because of its location Lloyd's coffeehouse attracted a clientele of ship owners, captains, merchants, and insurance brokers. The concept of marine insurance had been introduced to England earlier in the century, allowing owners of ships and cargos to mitigate the financial hit they took if a ship went down.

But, although insurance in the modern sense existed, insurance *companies* did not (Lloyd's today is still a peculiar hybrid, as noted below). A merchant with ship or cargo hired a broker to go from one wealthy individual to another, selling a share of the risk in return for a share of the premium. If nothing happened, the insurers got to keep the premium; if disaster struck, they were *personally* liable for their share of the claim . . . to the full extent of their personal fortunes, if necessary. Clearly, it was a field for people with a gambling instinct and a lot of money they could afford to risk.

Because of the amount of ship talk he heard, Edward Lloyd gained a reputation for being a trustworthy source of shipping news. His coffeehouse became recognized as the place to go to arrange for marine insurance. Lloyd himself was never directly involved in the insurance business, but he provided a congenial business atmosphere, semi-enclosed booths, and even writing materials for his patrons. His coffeehouse continued on after his death in 1713, and merchants continued to gather there.

For decades, a thin line separated those underwriters offering coverage in "respectable" marine underwriting from those betting on other things, like who would win a particular sports contest or war, or when the current king would die. Not wanting any longer to be associated with their seamier brethren, a number of the respectable brokers broke away in 1769 to set up their own coffeehouse in nearby Pope's Head Alley. They called it the "New Lloyd's Coffee House," and they allowed business dealings in marine insurance only.

The building proved too small, and so a committee was formed to find new premises. Seventy-nine brokers, underwriters, and merchants each chipped in £100 to finance new headquarters. When they moved this time, they left the coffee business behind. Nonetheless, their new headquarters were still referred to as Lloyd's Coffee House for decades afterward.

Over the following century, the Lloyd's society of underwriters evolved into its modern incarnation. They expanded to other kinds of insurance. By the 1990s, Lloyd's had grown to 32,000 members (called Names because they put their "name," or full reputation and worth, behind the risk), grouped into approximately 350 underwriting syndicates varying in size from a handful to a thousand. Each syndicate is managed by an agent and hires experts who determine the relative safety (and thereby the premium) for each insurance policy. As was the case three centuries ago, each Name is personally liable for claims, meaning that they can make money if things go well, but can lose their shirts if things go wrong. (Late in 1993, Lloyd's moved for the first time to allow corporations to join their underwriting ranks.)

Over time, Lloyd's has developed a generally well-deserved reputation for fairness, holding to a principal rule that no policyholder with a legitimate claim went unpaid. For example, after the disastrous San Francisco earthquake of 1906 that destroyed most of the city, every insurance company but one—Lloyd's—defaulted on their policies. In fact, when Lloyd's discovered that many of their policy holders had either fire insurance or earthquake insurance, but not both, Lloyd's leading underwriter cabled an unequivocal message to the company's San Francisco agent: "Pay all of our policyholders in full, irrespective of the terms of their policies."

Over the years, PR agents discovered that frivolous insurance policies with Lloyd's made for good publicity and that Lloyd's was a good sport about insuring just about anything. For example:

- Kid-show host Pinky Lee's lisp (a $50,000 policy)

- Betty Grable's legs ($1,000,000)

- Bruce Springsteen's voice (£3,500,000)

- A grain of rice with a tiny portrait of the Queen and the Duke of Edinburgh ($20,000)

- That Elvis wouldn't be found alive ($1,000,000)

- The beards of the Whisker's Club in Derbyshire against fire and "theft" (£20 each)

- A comedy troupe, against the risk of having members of the audience laugh themselves to death ($1,000,000)

- Skylab's disintegration and return to earth (£2,500,000 for property damage, £500,000 for deaths)

- The world's largest cigar (£17,933.35)

- The body of underwear model Suzanne Mizzi (£10,000,000)

- That the Loch Ness monster wouldn't be captured (£1,000,000)

This Sugar Daddy's No Sucker for Commies

What does a caramel on a stick have to do with fighting the international communist conspiracy? Plenty.

Robert Henry Winborne Welch, Jr., was born in 1899 and quickly got the reputation as a child prodigy. At the age of twelve, he entered the University of North Carolina and was, by his own admission years later, "the most insufferable little squirt that ever tried to associate with his elders." Raised as a fundamentalist Baptist, he tried to get his fellow students to come to Bible classes in his dorm room.

After four years, he entered the U.S. Naval Academy for two years before dropping out. He then entered Harvard Law School. Already a hard-line conservative, Welch left Harvard in the middle of his third and final year "in disgust over what Felix Frankfurter was teaching—that labor and management were enemies." While Professor Frankfurter went on to a distinguished stint on the Supreme Court, the embittered Welch went home and began a candy company, "the one field in which it seemed least impossible to get started without either capital or experience."

His Oxford Candy Company started making fudge from a recipe Welch bought from a candy store owner. He also made caramels. One day, inspired by the lollipop, he rolled out some of his caramels and stuck a stick into them. He called his new taste treat Papa Sucker. Powered by this success, the Oxford Candy Company did well enough for him to hire an employee, his brother James.

Not long after the Brach Candy Company offered to buy

the Papa Sucker brand. Robert worked out an unusual rights deal: They could make Papa Suckers ... but so could the Oxford Candy Company.

Things went along well enough for a while, but in 1925 James left and started his own candy company. In 1932, the Oxford company, hit hard by the Depression, went bankrupt. However, the James O. Welch Company was doing fine, so, in a reversal of fortunes, James hired his brother to take charge of advertising and sales. Robert, to avoid legal problems with Brach, changed his Papa Sucker's name to Sugar Daddy. His brother's company began selling it along with Robert's new candy lines of Sugar Babies, Junior Mints, and Pom Poms. In the next three decades, the company's annual sales increased from $200,000 to $20 million. Robert retired in 1956, a multi-millionaire.

But he was a very worried multimillionaire. There were foreign philosophies floating through the land that threatened his fortune and sense of well-being. "There is no reason on Earth why we should let ourselves be infected by such diseases as socialism and communism, and other ideological cancers," he wrote. In 1958, Welch decided to start an organization to wake America up to the grave dangers that threatened from every direction. He joined with ten other men and started the ultraconservative John Birch Society, named after an army intelligence agent who was killed in China ten days after World War II ended. Welch decided that Birch was the first casualty in World War III, which, as far as Welch was concerned, had already begun.

Welch believed that all Americans fell into one of four categories: "Communists, communist dupes or sympathizers, the uninformed who have yet to be awakened to the communist danger, and the ignorant." He believed it was almost too late to shake Americans out of their stupor: Wasn't America already ruled by Dwight David Eisenhower, "a dedicated, conscious agent of the communist conspiracy"? Was not democracy itself nothing more than "a deceptive phrase, a weapon of demagoguery and a perennial fraud"? It was the Birch Society, he believed, that would bring America back to "less government, more responsibility and, with God's help, a better world."

But, of course, it wouldn't be easy. Welch made up a map of the world, coloring each nation various shades of pink and red to indicate how "communistic" it was. The United States was a deep pink, and even the most brutal right-wing Latin American dictatorships that machine-gunned suspected communists by the carload were painted a light pink ("somewhat communistic") instead of white ("completely free of communism").

The John Birch Society achieved a surprising level of public awareness and a claimed membership in the high five figures. During the paranoid 1950s and 1960s, Welch and his cronies funded scores of books, started bookstores all over the country, published a monthly called *American Opinion*, and even opened a dozen summer camps to indoctrinate kids against communism. Welch used some of his Sugar Daddy earnings to buy billboards all over the country with the message "Impeach Earl Warren," the chief justice of the Supreme Court, who Welch believed was leading the country down a crimson path with pro-union and civil rights rulings.

Welch was also opposed to the fluoridation of water ("a communist plot to make Americans into mongolian idiots"), Norway ("secretly communist"), the Beatles ("their songs are written by a communist think tank"), federal aid to education, arms negotiations of all sorts, foreign aid, income taxes, collective bargaining, Social Security, and much more. He wasn't even particularly happy when Ronald Reagan was elected president, considering him hopelessly liberal.

As Welch's political analysis ripened to full flagrant paranoia, he eventually decided that the "international communist conspiracy" was itself merely a front for something even bigger and scarier. The "inner circle that has been running the show," all over the globe for two centuries, he became convinced, is a Masonic group formed in Bavaria in May 1776 that calls itself the Illuminati.

Welch died in 1985, and his organization is ailing and in debt. The fall of the Berlin Wall and communism in Eastern Europe has made it difficult for most the world to take its message seriously (even though, the Society claims, "the so-called fall of communism was just a clever hoax"). Even a move to Appleton, Wisconsin, to be close to the birthplace of hero Joseph McCarthy hasn't sufficiently bolstered the troops.

James Welch disavowed his brother's views in 1961. He sold his candy company to Nabisco in 1963, but continued as a Nabisco director until 1978. Like his brother, James died in 1985, just twenty-seven days after his brother.

Coincidence? Or was David Rockefeller, the Trilateral Commission, and the Bavarian Illuminati somehow involved? Thinking Americans want to know.

When You Care Enough to Send a $1.50 Card . . .

> *These kittens feel important*
> *'Cause here's what they get to do—*
> *They get to bring this birthday wish*
> *Especially "fur" you.*

The style is instantly recognizable—what could this poem be but the inscription of a Hallmark card? This one, featuring the world's cutest kittens on the front, is one of the company's all-time best sellers. It was written decades ago by the company's founder, Joyce C. Hall.

Hall was the youngest son of a devoutly religious Nebraskan woman who named him after a Methodist bishop, Isaac W. Joyce. Although mercilessly teased about his feminine first name, he didn't use his middle name, Clyde, because he thought it was even worse. He finally settled on J.C.

Hall's father, a traveling preacher, abandoned his wife and children when J.C. was nine. Hall began taking on odd jobs selling perfume, sandwiches, and lemonade to help support the family. Eventually Hall and his two older brothers found a market in selling imported postcards, which had become popular for correspondence and seasonal greetings.

In 1910, Hall dropped out of high school a semester short of graduation and took a train to Kansas City, where he tried a desperate ploy to increase his postcard business. In the YMCA room that was both his home and office, he put together hundred-packs of postcards and mailed them unbidden with invoices to shopkeepers throughout the Midwest.

Some of the dealers sent him back his postcards with blistering letters about his shady trick. Others just kept the cards without paying. But about one shopkeeper in three sent him a check, enough to have made the ploy worthwhile. Within a few months, Hall had socked away $200 in a local bank.

J.C. wrote to his brother Rollie, who moved into Hall's executive suites in the Kansas City YMCA. They formed Hall Brothers, acting as distributors of cards that were manufactured by other companies. The company became successful enough to move into new quarters.

Things went well enough until January 1915. Their warehouse was full of Valentines ready to ship. All those passionate messages in one place apparently caused spontaneous combustion. The whole building went up in flames, leaving the brothers without inventory and $17,000 in debt.

Reeling from disaster, the Halls decided to change the focus of the company. Rather than merely distribute cards, they were going to start manufacturing them as well. Somehow they convinced a banker to lend them enough money to buy an engraving company that had been one of their suppliers. They began designing and printing their own cards, shifting away from postcards and into the envelope-contained variety. With a line filled with sentimental illustrations and syrupy inscriptions, they expressed the feelings of a tongue-tied nation. Hall Brothers became the biggest greeting card company in the world.

In 1954, J.C. changed the name of the company to Hallmark, both as an indicator of quality and a nifty pun on his last name. One of his vice presidents was credited with coining the slogan "When You Care Enough to Send the Very Best," leaving off the logical conclusion ". . . But Not Enough to Actually Send a Present."

Hall, bucking a truism in the industry that advertising

doesn't sell greeting cards, had been buying time on radio since 1938. When television appeared, he thought it had great potential—but hated what he saw. He decided that Hallmark should sponsor quality broadcasting, always in the period before a major card-sending holiday (Christmas, Valentine's Day, Mother's Day, Easter). The result was the Hallmark Hall of Fame, an occasional showcase presenting drama, theater (it sponsored the first Shakespeare play presented in prime time), and even opera (*Amahl and the Night Visitors* was commissioned by NBC and given its first performance on the Hallmark Hall of Fame in 1951).

Hall died in 1982, leaving us with lots of rhyming sentiments and these words of wisdom from his biography, *When You Care Enough*: "If a man goes into business with only the idea of making a lot of money, chances are he won't. But if he puts service and quality first, the money will take care of itself. Producing a first-class product that is a real need is a much stronger motivation for success than getting rich."

Since Hall's death, the company has been embroiled in a few embarrassing scraps, including lawsuits and charges of unfair competition from small alternative card companies and retailers. One lawsuit claimed that Hallmark copied the distinctive look and feel of the company's cards. Other complaints said that Hallmark threatened to pull their cards from retailers who dared sell any other company's cards.

Meanwhile, Hallmark holds a fearsome share of the market, accounting for 44 percent of all greeting cards sold in the United States (some are disguised as other lines, like Shoebox and Ambassador). Hallmark produces more than 11 million cards a *day* in 13,000 different designs (as well as 5,000 noncard products like gift wrap and Christmas decorations). The cards are generated by a staff of 700 writers and illustrators, and helped out by 70,000 unsolicited ideas that pour in from consumers every year.

Women buy 80 to 85 percent of their greeting cards. Real men resist, but when there's no way out of it, they tend to buy the most expensive ones.

People question whether Hallmark's saccharine sentiments can continue glowing sunnily in an era of divorce, dysfunctional families, and abuse survivors. It looks like it. Apparently, the more society disintegrates, the more opportunities for a Hallmark greeting. The company now makes divorce announcements, reconciliation cards, pet-death sympathy cards, and even ambivalent Mother's Day cards that sidestep around traditional hearts and flowers sentiments ("I'm sorry if I haven't always shown it, but I do care about you . . . ").

But just in case future success isn't in the cards, Hallmark has also gobbled up Binney & Smith, the Crayola and Silly Putty company, and diversified heavily into real estate.

Why Baskin-Robbins Has 31 Flavors

Irvine Robbins's parents owned the Olympic Dairy in Tacoma, Washington, and manufactured ice cream with whatever surplus the family operation had. The Robbinses tried retailing their ice cream in grocery stores, but found that it didn't sell very well there. So they opened their own store.

Irvine began working there as a kid in the 1930s, out of a sense of family duty—and because he enjoyed the atmosphere. "Everybody who walked in that store was in a happy frame of mind," he said. "In conventional stores, everybody's in a hurry and yelling and screaming, but in the ice cream story everyone was coming in for fun. I finished a day's work happy."

But it wasn't always fun. One weekend when he was seventeen, he wanted to go out on an outing with friends and asked his father for the day off. "He was a stern old gent," said Irvine. "He said, 'I'll tell you what: You work while they play and a day will come that you'll play while they work.'"

After high school, Robbins went off to the University of Washington to study Political Science. Upon graduation, in wartime 1942, he joined the army.

When World War II ended, Robbins had to figure out what to do next. He decided that the last thing he wanted to do was go back to Tacoma, figuring that his father would put him to work as soon as he got home. He headed south to San Jose, California, with plans of opening an ice cream store of his own. He had saved about $6,000 and began scouting out locations in the San Francisco Bay area, but couldn't find a location he liked.

After looking for about a month, he decided to take a

weekend break in Los Angeles. Early Monday morning, he got up to drive back up to the Bay Area. Like many visitors to the area, however, he got lost trying to leave L.A.

Trying to find his bearings, he saw a sign that said "Two Blocks to Forest Lawn." He knew that Forest Lawn was the final resting place of hundreds of celebrities. In no big hurry to get home, he decided to make a stop.

Unfortunately, it was before 9:00 A.M., so Forest Lawn hadn't opened yet. Robbins decided to get a cup of coffee. Driving down quiet streets in the Los Angeles suburb of Glendale, he suddenly saw an empty storefront with a "For Rent" sign in the window. Another sign said to inquire at the rattan shop next door, which also opened at 9:00. Robbins waited around. Before noon he had rented the storefront.

Encouraged by his father, Robbins decided that there was no way to make any significant money with only one store. He started renting more storefronts and opening new stores. Meanwhile, his brother-in-law, Burton Baskin, got out of the service and decided to leave his prewar haberdashery business in Chicago and move to the Golden West. Robbins encouraged him to get into the ice cream business, too. They decided to work quasiseparately until they got enough stores, when they'd open their own ice cream factory to supply both chains. By 1948, Robbins had five "Snowbird" stores and Baskin had three "Burton's."

But under the apparently successful operations, there was a serious problem: They weren't making any money. "It was just damned lucky that I never took a course in accounting," Robbins liked to joke, "because if I had, I would have realized that I was broke. As it was, I didn't know it, and I kept right on going."

The problem is that ice cream stores require a lot of individual attention and supervision. The two owners with eight stores between them spent most of their time in a central office. They began losing touch with the retail operation. Baskin and Robbins realized that hired managers in the local stores could never have the same commitment that an owner would have.

That's when the idea struck them: Since we've got the factory to keep us busy, let's sell the stores to our managers. We'll sell them the ice cream and let them give the personal attention that the stores need to succeed. This was the first time a franchise system had been used in the food business, and Baskin and Robbins began selling rights to their ice cream stores all over the country. Later Ray Kroc (who had, coincidentally, been their milkshake mixer sales rep in the early days) would take the same basic idea and make a huge success of it with McDonald's, spawning dozens of other franchise schemes.

Baskin and Robbins then put their attention toward coming up with a tremendous variety of flavors, figuring that people could get chocolate, vanilla, and strawberry anywhere—but how about pumpkin pie or blueberry cheesecake or cantaloupe?

The "31 Flavors" slogan came when they hired the Carson-Roberts Advertising Agency in 1953. One of the agency people asked what differentiated Baskin & Robbins from its competitors. The answer was the variety of flavors. "We have a flavor for every day of the month," said Robbins. "Thirty-one flavors."

"That's it!" they all agreed. They changed the name of the company to Baskin-Robbins 31, hoping for the success of Heinz 57. Today, the company has many more flavors than that to choose from—well over 500 at last count—allowing them to rotate flavors from month to month. But they are always open to new ideas. In fact, some of their best flavor ideas are from customers who write or call their toll-free number with suggestions.

How Air Jordans Led to Shoe Inflation

In the old days sports shoes were called tennies and cost a lot less than good dress shoes. Both of these things changed with the Nike Air running-shoe lines.

The air-filled shoe wasn't Nike's idea. In fact, it wasn't even new. The first air sole was patented in the United States in 1882, the first of more than seventy different air-filled shoes that were registered with the U.S. Patent Office. Almost all of them, however, failed because of technical or commercial problems.

In 1969, Frank Rudy left a job at Rockwell International during a downturn in the aerospace industry. He had been the director of new products at Rockwell and decided that there was no reason why he had to hurry back into corporate life: He could come up with new products of his own in the garage of his Southern California home.

Actually, he wished he could be a ski bum, but his mortgage and family made that dream impractical. Instead, he started thinking about ski equipment. He decided his first new product would be an improved ski boot, most of the current models being, in his opinion, unnecessarily uncomfortable. He was joined in his quest by another Rockwell refugee named Bob Bogert, who had been an aerospace designer.

In a few years, they came up with a practical air-filled boot liner. They took it to Howard Head, owner of Head Skis, who licensed the design and began manufacturing boots with air soles inside. Unfortunately, not long afterward, he sold Head Skis to the AMF company. AMF decided to discontinue the new design.

Meanwhile, the recreational running trend began taking hold. Rudy and Bogert decided to design a running shoe model of their air sole, figuring that the air would absorb some of the pavement shock that long-distance runners were complaining about. After many attempts, they successfully designed a thin polyurethane air bag for the inside of running shoes and convinced the Bata shoe company to try them out.

The first prototypes worked great. The company ordered fifty more. Unfortunately, the oil embargo of 1974 was in full swing, and their supplier, without telling them, changed the formula for its polyurethane to use less oil. The new formula wasn't as strong as the old one. When the soles warmed up, the air inside expanded . . . and the sole exploded with a sound like a rifle shot. Bata suddenly lost interest.

Desperate and nearly broke, Rudy flew to France to meet with executives at shoe giant Adidas. But talks broke down over terms and whether it was technically possible to mass produce shoes with air inside. Then a fortuitous thing happened: While hanging around the offices, Rudy heard an Adidas employee mention a little company in America named Nike that was selling a lot of running shoes on the West Coast. Rudy made some calls, found out that there was a running shoe trade show going on that weekend in Anaheim, and caught the next flight back to Southern California.

He stopped by the booth in Anaheim just as it was closing and found out the name of the company's president, Phil Knight. Rudy immediately found a pay phone and called Knight at the company's headquarters in Beaverton, Oregon. Knight listened to Rudy's story and invited him to Nike headquarters.

Knight had started Nike a few years before. It had begun as Blue Ribbon Sports, distributing Tigers, an inexpensive Japanese running shoe. With time, Knight decided to start manufacturing his own shoes. An associate suggested the name

Nike, after the winged Greek goddess of victory. Knight didn't like it much, but it was better than the other names they came up with (among them Falcon, Bengal, and Dimension 6). At least the four-letter name fit on the shoes and complemented the winged logo design that he had bought from a Portland State art student for thirty-five dollars.

After years of struggling, Nike was finally making big strides in the recreational shoe business. Knight, an amateur runner, had seen the jogging and running boom coming and recognized the need for specialized and exotic shoes. He took Rudy's air-filled shoes for a run. They slowly deflated as he ran, but he saw the potential. "It was a great ride while it lasted," he told Rudy and put him on retainer for six months to see if he could make a success out of his idea.

Nike eventually decided that air soles were impractical. Sure, the air cushioned the road, but the friction from running heated the air to a level of discomfort and caused blisters. They tried putting an inflated midsole between a traditional sole and the runner's foot, which worked better.

They rushed the design into production. When the new shoe, called the Tailwind, hit the market, problems immediately started showing up. First of all, they were priced at $50 a pair, higher than any mass-produced running shoe up to that time. Then a last-minute fabric switch resulted in an expensive shoe that fell apart quickly, naturally infuriating customers. From the first run of the air shoes, just about half were returned as defective.

But serious runners quickly saw that there was some potential there. An in-house study found that the air midsoles reduced impact by about 10 percent and decreased energy use by 2.8 percent. Some runners patched their disintegrating shoes with duct tape and kept on running. And even though the air shoes became a sensitive subject around Nike headquarters for a while, the company eventually got the bugs out. They prepared to promote the shoes to the general public.

They got their chance when they signed a rookie basketball player named Michael Jordan. Nike actually signed him to save money—they had been signing up pros at anywhere from $8,000 to $100,000 each to wear and endorse their shoes. One day in 1983, they did an analysis and found they "owned" about half of the players in the NBA—at a cost of millions of dollars a year. Throughout all sports, they had two thousand expensive athletes on their endorsement roster.

They decided to find one promising rookie who had the potential to become a superstar and put all their eggs in his basket early, before he had a chance to get too expensive. Charles Barkley was one candidate. Patrick Ewing was another. But the company finally settled on twenty-year-old college junior Michael Jordan. They decided that they would design a brand new shoe for him, push it hard, and tie the product to the man and vice versa, so that when consumers saw the player, they thought "shoes!"

Nike offered Jordan $2.5 million for a five-year contract, plus royalties on every Air Jordan shoe sold (they didn't call them Jordan Airs to avoid confusion with a Mideast airline and Elvis Presley's longtime backup group).

Nike came up with a proposed shoe, logo, and advertising campaign. There was only one stumbling block: Jordan didn't particularly like Nike shoes. In fact, he loved Adidas and was willing to make concessions to get an endorsement contract with them. He told their representatives, "You don't even have to match Nike's deal—just come close," but they offered only $100,000 a year, with no special Jordan shoe and no royalties.

In August 1984, Jordan signed with Nike. Nike came up with a distinctive black and red design for him. In fact, the design was so distinctive that NBA commissioner David Stern threatened to fine Jordan $1,000 if he wore the shoes during a game because they violated the NBA "uniformity of uniform" clause. He wore them anyway, creating an uproar in the stands and in the press ("Michael Jordan is not the most incredible, the most colorful, the most amazing, the most flashy, or the most mind-boggling thing in the NBA," wrote Chicago *Journal* sportswriter Steve Aschberner the next day. "His shoes are.")

Nike gladly paid Jordan's fine. It was the beginning of a brilliant PR and advertising campaign. Air Jordans went on to become the most successful athletic endorsement in history, selling over $100 million worth of the shoes in the first year alone. The dark side: Air Jordans became so popular that it became dangerous to wear them in some cities as teenagers began killing other teenagers for their $110 sneakers.

Incidentally, despite the name, Air Jordan soles don't have air in them. They contain a gas that has larger molecules than air so it doesn't leak through the airbag material as easily.

More Business Wisdom from the Sages

Here's the rule for bargains: "Do other men, for they would do you." That's the true business precept.
—Charles Dickens, 1812–1870

The business of America is business.
—Calvin Coolidge, 1872–1933

There is nothing more requisite in business than dispatch.
—Joseph Addison, 1672–1719

Life without industry is guilt, and industry without art is brutality.
—John Ruskin, 1819–1900

If you have great talents, industry will improve them: if you have but moderate abilities, industry will supply their deficiency.
—Sir Joshua Reynolds, 1723–1792

Grace is given of God, but knowledge is bought in the market.
—Arthur Hugh Clough, 1819–1861

Polaroid Schizophrenia

There are Polaroid cameras and there are Polaroid sunglasses. So how are these two Polaroid products connected? And how can it be that you can buy a Polaroid lens for your regular camera—will they somehow make it develop photos in a minute? And how does 3-D come into all this? It's enough to make you a Polaroid schizophrenic.

The name Polaroid was coined in 1934 by Smith College professor Clarence Kennedy to describe a plastic material created by techno-genius Edwin Herbert Land. But Land himself wasn't sure he liked the name. He was leaning toward Epibollipol (supposedly Greek for "sheet polarizer"), but thankfully, a friend talked him out of it.

Land had been struck by inspiration eight years earlier at age seventeen. He was strolling down Broadway in New York City, on vacation from Harvard, and was blinded by the lights of an on-coming car. The boy scientist had been reading theoretical studies about polarized light. Normally, light waves travel in a forward motion, vibrating at right angles in every direction from the direction of the forward path. Polarization makes light waves go in a parallel plane instead of vibrating in every which direction. Land wondered if he could develop a low-cost polarized lens that would cut the glare from headlights without reducing their effectiveness at illuminating the road.

Other scientists had discovered the phenomenon of polarization using crystals. One, William Bird Herapath, an English physician, actually produced polarizing material in 1852 after theorizing that tiny needle-shaped crystals would "comb" light. He knew that such crystals could be formed by combining iodine with quinine salt, so he dosed a student's dog with a huge dose of quinine. To the dog's quinine-rich urine, he added iodine. Sure enough, he found that the tiny, very fragile crystals that formed could be seen to be polarizers if you looked at them under a microscope. Herapath spent the rest of his career fruitlessly trying to create a larger and stronger polarizing crystal (maybe if he had tried dosing an elephant?) until his death seventy years later.

Land, his work cut out for him, decided that the quest to make a simple and inexpensive polarizer was a matter that was worth his time and considerable intellect. He didn't go back to Harvard at the end of his vacation; he stayed in New York, settling into a small apartment to figure out the problem.

By day, Land haunted the library and read everything he could find about Herapath and polarization. By night, he worked in secrecy in a science lab building at Columbia University. There was a reason for his secrecy—he didn't belong there. He climbed the fire escape each night to a window that was left unlocked and took advantage of the unusually well-equipped laboratory.

"It is a curious property of research activity," Land once said, "that after the problem has been solved, the solution usually seems obvious." His solution was that Herapath had gone off on a wrong path: Rather than trying to find one large crystal to work as a filter, why not align millions of microscopic crystals in rows like a comb to form an "optical grain" that would do the same thing?

Land's parents agreed to fund his quest and even provided enough money to hire an assistant, a former dental technician named Ernest Calabro who performed tasks of plating, cutting, and polishing alloy and glass plates without having any idea of what the secretive Land was up to. For his part, Land believed he would solve the problem within a relatively short time, perhaps a few months.

It was more like three years, but he finally got the solution that had eluded Herapath. He used a powerful electromagnet to line up millions of tiny iodine-quinine crystals in a hollow glass cylinder. Shining a light through it confirmed that he had succeeded. He soon figured out how to do the same thing on a plastic sheet, with one thousand billion crystals per square inch. In 1929, at the age of twenty, Land had his first major invention.

About that same time, the stock market crashed, reversing his family's fortunes. Land returned to Harvard, aware that his family was sacrificing to keep him there, and began working on his degree in dead earnest. Land also continued his research, this time using a lab provided to him by a professor. His research became so compelling that he dropped out of Harvard one semester shy of graduating and never returned.

He spent the next several years trying to interest carmakers in the safety features of Polaroid windshields and headlights. To remind himself of what he was trying to accomplish, Land mounted a sign in his laboratory that said, "Every night, 50 people will die on the highway from headlight glare." But the carmakers believed that styling and horsepower sold cars and that safety features actually were a mistake because they reminded potential buyers that a car could be a dangerous thing. So even though the Polaroid materials would have added only about four dollars to the cost of producing a car and could have saved thousands of lives, Detroit turned Land down.

Other manufacturers, however, started seeing some applications for Land's new material. Out of the blue, future competitor Kodak sent a huge order for something that didn't even exist yet—a Polaroid lens to tone down glare and sky light for photos. Movie makers started looking into polarized lenses and glasses for 3-D movies. (Unfortunately, 3-D was set back for a decade when Land demonstrated it to Harry Warner of Warner Bros. "I don't get it," said Harry after the movie, "what's the big deal?" It wasn't until several weeks later that Land found out from a Hollywood friend that Warner had a glass eye.)

Wurlitzer began using Polaroid film for light displays on its new jukeboxes. The American Optical Company bought the right to make Polaroid sunglasses. And with war at hand, the Polaroid company received millions of dollars in contracts to develop optical military applications. By war's end, the Polaroid Company's sales had multiplied to $17 million.

But well before that, Land began getting bored and restless. He began looking for new scientific problems to take on. In 1943, while photographing vacation scenes in Santa Fe, his three-year-old daughter asked to see the pictures he just took. When he explained that she couldn't see them until they got home, she wanted to know, "Why not?"

Why not indeed? Why did people have to wait for their photos? It shouldn't be that complicated.

Land was immediately struck by the idea of instant photography. Before the day was over, he had already worked out the basic process. The developing chemicals would have to be included in the film pack, maybe in small pods that would rupture when the film traveled through a roller system like those on an old-fashioned washing machine.

Land went back to his lab and started working with a team of technicians, including Maxfield Parrish, Jr., son of the artist. Four years later, they had a working model to demonstrate and began production. A year later, they introduced the camera in department stores, accompanied by near riots. People had never seen anything like this camera. They snapped it up, even at the outrageous price of $89.75 in 1948 dollars—the equivalent of over $500 today.

ory. He bought seven dollars' worth of ice, salt water, and an electric fan. Sure enough, he found that slow freezing allowed large ice crystals to form, bursting the food's cell walls. Fast freezing prevented that, saving the cellular integrity, and thus the texture and flavor, for months on end. As a side benefit, he also found that he could entertain dinner guests by bouncing frozen steaks off the kitchen floor before cooking them for dinner.

In 1923, Birdseye gambled everything he owned designing a practical large-scale fast freezer and setting up Birdseye Foods, Inc. He nearly went broke. When the Postum Company (which changed its name to General Foods that same year) offered to buy his patented process for $22 million, Birdseye jumped at the chance.

The corporation already had a distribution system set up, the lack of which had been Birdseye's undoing. It also could afford to buy advertising to convince America that it needed frozen food. By 1934, 80 percent of the frozen food market belonged to General Food's Birds Eye Division. (They added the space in Birdseye's name and began pronouncing it like it was spelled.)

For his part, Birdseye went on tinkering, amassing over 250 patents on a range of things from recoilless harpoons to a way to turn sugar cane waste into paper. Like Bacon, he died with his inventor's boots on—in 1956, while in Peru trying to figure out how to make paper out of the agave plant, he had a fatal heart attack from the high altitude. But he had lived long enough to see the preeminent use for his fast-freezing process: the TV Dinner, invented by the Swanson brothers.

Gilbert and Clarke Swanson had a problem: They were surrounded by turkeys. *Real* turkeys. They owned the largest turkey processing plant in the country, C. A. Swanson & Sons, and it drove them crazy that most Americans ate turkey on

How TV Dinners Became Tray Chic

In our time, frozen dinners have become yupscale and preten tious. In those plastic trays you can get frozen items tha twenty years ago you'd have to go to a fancy French restauran for. The frozen portions are expensive, reasonably nutritiou: microwaveable . . . and about as tasty as airline fare. But wasn't always like that. There are those who say that the da} of the past were best, when the trays were aluminum, th choices were scanty (turkey, chicken, or Salisbury steak), ar today's "gourmet entree" was not too proud to call itself a "T dinner."

Frozen food in your local grocery is a relatively rece thing. True, seventeenth-century scientist Sir Francis Bac had some ideas about freezing as a preservative and even c some experiments that looked promising. (Unfortunately, died of hypothermia after spending a cold afternoon stuffi snow into a dead chicken.) But the modern-day frozen fc industry owes its existence to Clarence Birdseye, who p nounced his name BIRD-zee and liked to be called Bob.

Birdseye, a naturalist and writer of books on wildflow: birds and mammals, had gone to Labrador in 1917 to cond a survey of fish and wildlife for the U.S. government. W! there, he noticed that the Native Canadians' meat and pou didn't get mushy when frozen and thawed. It felt and ta: nearly fresh, unlike food he had tried freezing back in States.

He figured that it was because of the extreme cold, w! froze the food quicker. When he got back, he tested the only one day a year: Thanksgiving. The Swansons made it their goal to insinuate more turkey meat into America's diet. First they started making frozen turkey potpies. These became so popular that people started clamoring for more varieties. This was good news for business, but not good news for the turkey problem.

In 1951, the Swanson kitchens began experimenting with individual portion meals that could be popped into the oven and eaten without much preparation. Inspired by the segmented plates used in diners for blue plate specials, they made similar trays out of aluminum and put dinner courses in them.

Television was the hot new fad sweeping the country. The Swanson Company arranged to sponsor its own show, "Ted Mack's Family Hour." Gilbert Swanson invited some friends over to have dinner and watch the premier show.

While eating in front of Swanson's console TV, one of the guests remarked about how odd it was to see everybody balancing food trays on their laps in front of the TV. Swanson suddenly thought of the individual portion meals his company was working on. They'd be perfect for eating while watching TV, and tying them in to the TV craze couldn't hurt. In fact, if you rounded the corners of the aluminum trays, they'd sort of look like a TV screen . . . why not call them TV Dinners?

The next morning Gilbert told his brother about the idea. Clarke liked it, and suggested putting a picture of a TV on the box with the dinner coming off the screen.

In January 1952, the first Swanson's TV Dinners rolled off the line in Omaha. They contained turkey, cornbread stuffing, gravy, buttered peas, and sweet potatoes in orange and butter sauce—and cost 98¢. The dinners did well.

Soon the company introduced fried chicken TV Dinners, which sold quickly until consumers started noticing that the chicken tasted like bananas. It turned out that the yellow ink on the box used a solvent that smelled like bananas and that the smell was seeping into the food. Swanson recalled the chicken dinners and changed the ink, but one food chain in Florida complained because it said that its customers actually preferred the banana-flavored variety. Swanson pragmatically shipped its entire recalled inventory to Florida.

In the 1960s, after TV became a guilty pleasure instead of a harmless fad, Swanson's redesigned its package to downplay the TV Dinner brand name, allowing it to more or less become a generic term. In 1984, the Swanson Company replaced the aluminum tray with a microwaveable plastic one. As a sop to the health-consciousness times, the company replaced the brownie with a fruit dessert in 1986, but soon reversed the decision after a deluge of customer complaints.

We can hope that with a consumer crusade they might bring back the classic aluminum tray as well. The dinners don't quite taste the same without that faint metallic tinge to the vegetables. And if that works, maybe next we can work toward the return of that banana-flavored chicken.

God, Mammon, and Other Enlightened Quotes

The most beautiful sight we see is the child at labor; as early as he may get at labor, the more beautiful, the more useful does his life get to be.
—Coca-Cola magnate Asa Candler, arguing against proposed child labor laws in 1908

Jesus did not and does not propose to remove the inequalities of life. On the contrary, these inequities are a part of the divine order ordained by Him for the promoting of the brotherhood of man.

—Asa Candler, president of Coca-Cola

God runs Tiffany's.

—Walter Hoving, president of Tiffany's

If you have to pay money to have the right thing done, it is only just and fair to do it.
—Colis Huntington, Central Pacific Railroad, explaining his company's pay-offs of $1.9 million to legislators between 1862 and 1873

Corporations are people, too.

—Secretary of the Treasury William Simon advocating tax breaks for big business

I've always believed that what is good for the country is good for General Motors, and what's good for General Motors is good for the country.

—Charles E. Wilson, GM president

WD-40: Petroleum Distillate . . . or Elixir of the Gods?

WD-40, once considered just an alternative to light machine oil, has attracted a virtual cult following as a mechanical cure-all. Some people swear it works like a spray-on Holy Water, not just bringing machines back from the dead, but also soothing arthritis, attracting fish to bait, removing crayon stains, and more.

Where did this stuff come from? And how did it get the reputation of being so much more than it appears to be?

The story begins with the mysterious billionaire Howard Hughes, who inspired WD-40 by backing out of a deal. In 1952, Hughes ordered a number of Convair 880 passenger jets from General Dynamics of San Diego, California. After they were built he abruptly refused delivery.

While the two sides argued, the planes sat on a runway in San Diego. In the damp winter, parts of the planes started rusting. General Dynamics realized it had to do something before the planes were completely worthless. They called Rocket Chemical, a three-person company that specialized in making lubricants and such for the aerospace industry. President and head chemist Norman Larsen started working on a formula that would get under water and push it out of the microscopic pores in metal, protecting them from rust.

Larsen submitted a formula he thought would do the trick. General Dynamics rejected it. Larsen patiently submitted another . . . and another . . . and another. It took forty tries, so, with a chemist's literalness, Larsen called his formula WD (for Water Displacement)-40.

General Dynamics ordered barrels of the stuff. After successfully treating the planes, workers started using WD-40 on Atlas missile parts and skins as well. They found that it did a good job on almost anything that was prone to corrosion or that needed lubrication. Some started sneaking the stuff home, finding new uses for it. As General Dynamics workers transferred to other plants, they took containers of WD-40 with them. Word spread. Rocket Chemical started getting small orders from all over the country, along with ideas of what WD-40 could be used for.

Larsen suspected he had a potential consumer product on his hands. He started marketing small aerosol containers locally, and sold them by mail order. By 1960, his company had expanded to seven employees, including sales reps who sold the product from the trunks of their cars to nearby hardware and sporting goods stores.

In 1961, Hurricane Carla battered the Gulf Coast, and Larsen sent his entire stock of WD-40 to be used in reconditioning water-damaged vehicles and equipment. That same year, the company made the only modification ever to the formula—it added a light scent to hide the product's oily odor.

Rocket Chemical phased out its other industrial chemicals and changed its name to the WD-40 Company to reflect its only product. By 1993, it had grown to 140 employees in four countries. Annual sales are nearly $100 million, and the familiar little blue, yellow and red aerosol could be found in 77 percent of all American homes.

MIRACLE PANACEA

Sure, WD-40 works on squeaky metal parts, rusty tools and other things. But have you heard of any of these other uses that its fanatical followers swear are true?

• Masks human scent on fishing lures.

• Frees tongues that get stuck to frozen metal in winter.

• Removes gum, Silly Putty, and crayons from hair, carpeting, walls, and floors.

• Soothes arthritis.

• Stops shoes from squeaking.

• Cures mange on pets.

• Frees pets and children from that sticky mouse and cockroach trap paper.

• According to a man in Washington State, WD-40 keeps salmon from sticking to the barbecue grill. He skins the fish before eating it, but claims that WD-40 "imparts a wonderful flavor to the meat." (He apparently hasn't heard the recommendations about using less oil in cooking.)

• Another man found an even more unexpected use for WD-40. He knocked a burglar out by hitting him on the head with the can.

How Swatch Saved the Swiss Watch Industry

For centuries, the Swiss dominated the watch market with a product famous for reliability and craftsmanship. In the 1970s, however, the complacent Swiss watchmakers made a fateful decision: that making digital watches was below them.

They were probably right. Digital watches started as an expensive novelty, but it soon became clear that they could be stamped out much more cheaply than the traditional analog watch. Swiss watchmakers quickly ceded the low end of the watch market to upstart companies in Japan and Hong Kong that were producing digital "junk." They figured that most consumers would continue to demand the style and reliability of genuine Swiss watches.

But it didn't quite work that way. Seiko, Casio, and other Asian companies expanded their lines out of the low end and moved aggressively into the middle. While the Swiss continued to manufacture 97 percent of high-end watches (priced at $400 or more), by 1980 they had lost all of the low end (under $75) and all but 3 percent of the middle ($75 to $400).

The Swiss watch industry fell into a shambles, retreating on all fronts. The years of tradition, once a strength, turned into a liability. Not knowing what else to do, they went into denial and continued doing things the way they always had, waiting for watch consumers to come to their senses and start buying Swiss watches again.

It didn't happen. Hundreds of Swiss companies went bankrupt, sold out, or ended up in the hands of banks that didn't want them. As a result of this turmoil, Ernst Thomke was dragged back into the watch business.

Twenty years earlier, a teenage Thomke had been an apprentice watchmaker-mechanic at ETA, the parts-making arm of the country's biggest watch manufacturer, SMH, but he didn't stay long. Instead, he went back to school and earned a degree in chemistry and medicine at the University of Bern, went on to conduct tumor research for the Swiss government, and finally ended up in the Swiss branch of Beecham Industries, where he worked his way up from researcher to managing director.

But one day in 1978, completely out of the blue, he got a call from his old boss at ETA, who was now the company president. He was about to retire, he said, and he remembered what a good apprentice Thomke had been. He had nobody else who would or could pull the company out of its desperate straits, he said. Would Thomke considering coming back and taking over?

Thomke considered the complete absurdity of the request. He was in a comfortable, secure position where he was free to pursue his passion for airplanes, fast motorcycles, and flashy cars. He was being asked to leave it to take on a high-stress dawn-to-dusk job in a dying industry that he knew little about. Thomke thought it over and said yes.

He came into his new position determined to breathe new life into the company based on his experience in marketing and research. He was appalled to find how far his new employer lagged behind the Japanese in innovation. Ominously, the Japanese had begun moving into the high-end watch market with a much-ballyhooed ultrathin analog watch that made Swiss models look chunky and ungainly in comparison.

Thomke called his engineers together and challenged them to design a high-priced analog that would be thinner than two millimeters—in six months.

"To outsiders, the competition probably sounds silly and meaningless," Thomke said later, "but I wanted to position them to rethink their whole approach, to find new technical solutions and develop new modules and batteries. I also wanted to send a signal to the industry and make a statement on behalf of Swiss ingenuity."

The project was quickly dubbed "delirium tremens" by the engineers. Six months of arduous work resulted in more than meeting the challenge: They proudly presented Thomke with a one-millimeter-thick watch. The new watch had a revolutionary design: Instead of manufacturing the moving parts separately and placing them into the watch housing, the mechanism was built directly into the watch case. This not only reduced thickness, it eliminated several complicated steps in building the watch. The company named the new watch the Delirium and rushed it to the market by the end of the year. It was a tremendous success, with five thousand sold at a price of about $4,700 each.

On the heels of this success, Thomke decided to go after the digital watchmakers on their own turf. He issued a new challenge to his engineers: Design an analog watch that will cost less than 10 Swiss francs ($6.65) to produce.

The engineers came back after two weeks to respectfully tell him that he was completely out of his mind. The least expensive watch mechanism (called the "movement" in the watch trade) by itself cost 25 francs to make, and he was asking for a complete watch, including case and strap. Impossible!

"They said it couldn't be done," recalled Thomke, "and that was almost the end of it, because this is an industry run by engineers." But a pair of engineers, Jacques Muller and Elmar Mock, volunteered that they'd be willing to try the impossible.

Building on what they had learned from working on the Delirium, the two figured out a way to reduce the number of movement parts from ninety to fifty-one. They created a plastic watch case that could be used as the watch's mounting plate, allowing a 40 percent reduction in cost over conventional watch assemblies.

They started looking at labor costs next. Watch movements were traditionally mounted on a plate and then placed into the watch cases, requiring turning the watch over several times and securing the loose parts during assembly. That was expensive and time consuming. Mock and Muller figured out a way to stack the parts directly into the case from the top only, then weld the watch case shut with a laser beam (while this made the watch impossible to repair, it also made it waterproof to a depth of 100 feet). They designed a factory that used a good deal of automation. Still, traditional Swiss quality was attended to: The parts were made to one-five-hundredth of a millimeter tolerance and the plastic cases were designed to withstand quite a bit of abuse.

Most importantly, Mock and Muller met Thomke's 10 franc goal. On July 1, 1980, they walked triumphantly into Thomke's office to show him their design. Thomke immediately got to work on test marketing, getting the new watch into production, mapping out advertising, and coming up with a name. The promotion people in the company began thinking of designer-fantasy names and had a list of about twenty of them. But then SMH's American ad agency, McCann-Erickson, contracted "Swiss watch" into "Swatch," and the name stuck.

It became clear that the plastic case would allow a great deal of flexibility in design and color, allowing a whimsical attitude that could be aimed at the target market of teens and twenties. That became one of the keys to the success of the watch—the relative cheapness could allow people to collect different Swatches to match their moods, wardrobes, and activities.

The first Swatch came out for forty dollars in 1983. (This price has remained constant for the basic Swatch for more than ten years.) The company launched it in an audacious manner. They built a giant working Swatch model 500 feet high, weighing 13 tons, and hung it from outside the tallest skyscraper in Frankfurt, Germany.

Every year Swatch releases 140 strikingly different designs as well as occasional limited edition pressings. Over 100 million Swatches—depicting everything from kid's book illustrations to fish to a plate of bacon and eggs—had been sold. A coterie of collectors has sprung up around the product, selling and trading unusual and early editions for many times the original price. And even self-avowed noncollectors collect them anyway—the average owner has more than three Swatches.

Nicholas Hayek, chief executive officer of SMH, told the *Harvard Business Review* that the Swatch story had two lessons:

First, it is possible to build high-quality, high-value, mass-market consumer products in a high-wage country at low cost. Notice I said *build*, not just design and sell. We build all of our Swatches in Switzerland, where the most junior secretary earns more than the most senior engineer in Thailand or Malaysia. . . . We are all global companies competing in global markets. But that does not mean we owe no allegiance to our own societies. . . . We must build where we live. When a country loses the know-how and expertise to manufacture things, it loses its capacity to create wealth and its financial independence. . . . We have to change the reflex, the instinctive reaction that if a company has a mass-market consumer product, the only place to build it is Asia or Mexico. CEOs must say to their people "We will build this product in our country at a lower cost and with higher quality than anywhere else in the world." And they have to figure out how to do it.

The second lesson is related to the first. You can build mass-market products in countries like Switzerland or the United States only if you embrace the fantasy and imagination of your childhood and youth. People may laugh—the CEO of a huge Swiss company talking about fantasy. But that's the real secret behind what we have done. It's an unusual attitude for Switzerland—or any other part of Europe. We kill too many good ideas by rejecting them without thinking about them, by laughing at them. Ten years ago, the people on the original Swatch team asked a crazy question: Why can't we design a striking, low-cost, high-quality watch and build it in Switzerland? The bankers were skeptical. A few suppliers refused to sell us parts. They said we would ruin the industry with this crazy product. But the team overcame the resistance and got the job done.

How Twinkies Got Cremed

They're golden brown, irresistibly spongy, and filled with "creme" (you don't think there's actually *cream* in there, do you?). And they're the Continental Baking Company's biggest seller, even beating out that other Continental food marvel, Wonder Bread. Twinkies are quite literally "the greatest thing since sliced bread," since Wonder was the first bread that came presliced and packaged.

Twinkies were invented in 1930 at the beginning of the Great Depression by the Chicago-area Continental plant manager. His name was James A. Dewar. At the time, Continental was a new company, only six years old, and Dewar wasn't completely confident in its ability to weather the new economic times. It didn't make sense to him, for example, that the plant had lots of expensive pans dedicated to a product called Little Short Cake Fingers that was baked for only six weeks a year. The fingers were designed to be made into strawberry shortcake, so the pans went into commission only during the strawberry season. During the rest of the year, they lay idle.

Dewar figured that the shortcake fingers could sell year-round if the company came up with something to replace the strawberry cream. He mixed up a banana-flavored "creme" and figured out a way to inject it into the shortcake using three syringelike injection tubes.

But Dewar was having trouble coming up with a name he liked until, on a business trip to St. Louis, he and a colleague drove past the Twinkle Toes Shoes factory. His friend suggested the name "Twinkle Fingers" for his new cakes; Dewar shortened it to Twinkies.

Continental started selling Dewar's new Twinkies in packs of two for five cents. Ten years later, the company switched from banana filling to vanilla. It has made at least 45 billion Twinkies—over 2 million tons of cakes. Sales records show that they are by far the best selling snack cake in the Midwest.

Because of their success, Twinkies have had plenty of critics who call them the archetypal junk food. TV's Archie Bunker damned them with dubious praise, calling them "the white man's soul food."

In the early 1970s, they were mentioned prominently in a song called "Junk Food Junkie" and they were accused, in what was called "the Twinkie defense," of mentally unbalancing a San Francisco supervisor to the point of committing murder.

The company responds blandly: "We make these cakes out of the same ingredients that you'd find in a typical kitchen," says a company spokesperson. "It's a fun food. That's our position."

Dewar, before he died in 1985, was a little less soft-spoken in defending his creation, "the best darn-tootin' idea I ever had." To live eighty-eight years like him, he advised that you should "eat Twinkies every day and smoke a pack of cigarettes." Seriously, he'd add, "Some people say that Twinkies are the quintessential junk food, but I fed them to my four kids and they feed them to my fifteen grandchildren. My boy Jimmy played football for the Cleveland Browns. My other son, Bobby, played quarterback for the University of Rochester. Twinkies never hurt them."

As to the legend that Twinkies will last forever on the grocery shelf, the company admits they have a long shelf life because the "creme" keeps them moist, but points out that unsold Twinkies are replaced in stores after only four to six days.

How the VW Bugged Detroit's Autocracy

The VW Beetle was America's first import and the first counterculture car. In the 1950s and 1960s, it was a way for Americans to vote with their dollars against the excesses of Detroit—especially its obsession with horsepower and styling instead of quality and engineering.

The Bug was designed by Ferdinand Porsche, the brilliant auto designer. Born in Austria in 1875 he fathered a succession of high-powered yet elegant autos, including the Mercedes, for a succession of German manufacturers.

He moved from company to company because his tactlessness matched his brilliance. His undisguised contempt for the shortsighted, budget-driven bean-counters who ran car companies did not endear him to management teams. Tired of working for them, he finally opened his own design firm.

Porsche was a great admirer of American automaker Henry Ford and dreamed of creating an inexpensive yet reliable "people's car," like Ford's Model T. In the 1930s, Porsche traveled to America to meet Ford and tour his factories. He told Ford of his plans and asked if he minded some competition. "If somebody can build a car better or cheaper than I can, that serves me right," answered Ford.

Porsche decided that his *volksauto* would have to be a completely new design, not just a stripped and scaled-down version of an existing car. He gave the car a reverse-teardrop shape to increase fuel efficiency. Brilliantly, he redesigned parts that were too heavy or expensive. Heavy wheel springs gave way to a new kind of suspension system that used torsion bars.

Porsche replaced the heavy chassis with a sheet-metal floor pan, creased and corrugated for strength. He mounted a small air-cooled engine in back of the car, which improved traction, cut the expense of the drive train, and did away with the space-wasting hump in the passenger compartment.

Porsche arranged for funding in 1932 from Zündapp, a motorcycle firm that was trying to diversify fast in the face of a worldwide depression that was hitting Germany especially hard. Zündapp advanced enough money for three handmade prototypes, but insisted that Porsche use an experimental five-cylinder engine the company had developed. This engine proved completely unsatisfactory. Porsche was also having trouble with his torsion bars (if the metal was too soft and flexible, the bars sagged; if too hard and brittle, they shattered with a resounding crack). After a while, Zündapp bowed out.

Porsche's project was adopted next by Stuttgart-based NSU, another desperate motorcycle firm interested in marketing a cheap car. Porsche solved the suspension problems and came up with a new four-cylinder engine that could power his car to speeds of up to 70 mph. In 1933, he built three prototypes. However, NSU decided to drop the project, deciding that the venture was too risky and its tooling costs too expensive. Besides, motorcycle sales were beginning to pick up again.

During this time, Adolf Hitler came to power. Hitler was an auto enthusiast, even though he had never learned to drive. He was an admirer of the Mercedes and Porsche racing cars, which were winning prestige for Germany in international races. Shortly after becoming chancellor, Hitler embarked on an ambitious program to upgrade German highways. He reduced licensing regulations and auto taxes and began making speeches encouraging automakers to come up with low-cost automobiles for workers. Industrious German workers, he thundered, should not have to walk or ride a bicycle; under National Socialism they will have *volkswagens*—people's autos—of their own!

Despite the exhortations, the conservative, upscale German auto industry did nothing, skeptical that such a car was economically feasible. Porsche, looking for a new backer, finally found one: the new German chancellor, Adolf Hitler. Hitler ordered the automaking industry association to hire the Porsche design office to develop a people's car to be priced at the equivalent of $360. The apolitical Porsche welcomed Hitler's support for his dream. In quick order, he produced thirty-three cars and ran them around test tracks. They racked up a total of 1.8 million miles without significant breakdowns.

Hitler figured he couldn't depend on the reluctant private sector. He decided that the government should make the car itself under the auspices of the *Gezuvor-Gesellschaft zur Vorbereitung des Deutschen Volkswagens GmbH*" (Society for the Development of the German People's Car).

On May 26, 1938, the Reich laid a foundation stone about 50 miles east of Hanover for the Volkswagenwerk, an ultramodern factory and city. Hitler announced that the car would henceforth be known as the *Kraft-durch-Freude Wagen* (Strength-Through-Joy Car).

Meanwhile, the government announced a savers program where citizens could contribute five or more reichsmarks a week in an auto prepayment plan. Reich coffers were enriched by $67 million as 336,668 Germans jumped at the chance of owning their own cars. Not that any of them actually got a car: Only 210 Strength-Through-Joy Cars were built. They were given to Nazi bigwigs before the factories were diverted to the war effort. Staffed by slave labor from the concentration camps, the wartime factory produced some 70,000 Jeeplike Kübelwagens and amphibious Schwimmkübels, various aircraft parts, and sheet-metal stoves for soldiers on the Eastern Front. (After the war, lawsuits by savers groups resulted in a 1961 settlement consisting of either a significant credit toward buying a new VW, or a lesser amount of cash.)

The Volksvagenwerk factory, a target of allied bombers, was in shambles when captured by the Americans in April 1945. The factory was scheduled for dismantling, but a few of the former car workers—hungry, having nothing much to do, and remembering the dream of volkswagen prosperity—started coming in to see what was left of the production line. They located tools and dies, scrounged materials, and managed to hand-build a few Strength-Through-Joy Cars. These they bartered to the occupying British officers for food.

The British encouraged the efforts, both as a source of vehicles and as a way to provide jobs for the restless and hungry townspeople. Soon VW workers began searching far and wide for raw materials, "buying" them with a completed car or two. By the end of the year, six thousand people worked at the plant—half building cars, the other half repairing roofs, walls, and machinery—and they produced 1,785 cars. The following year, the still-unmanaged workers raised production to 10,020 cars.

Then production started sagging. In 1947, the factory produced only 8,987 cars, including the first VWs ever earmarked for export—fifty-six sedans bought by Ben Pon of the Netherlands. It was clear that the plant could not continue building cars in an uncapitalized, unmanaged plant that used only scrounged materials.

The occupying English army tried to get British carmakers to take the plant over, but the Brits turned up their noses at the little car they described as ugly, noisy, outlandish, and unsalable. It was offered for free to Henry Ford II. He turned down the offer on the recommendation of his CEO, Ernest Breech, who told him, "Mr. Ford, I don't think that what we are being offered here is worth a damn!" The Soviet Government, noting that the zone they controlled started less than five miles east of the factory, offered to readjust borders westward and take the VW problem off the hands of the Allies. The Allies declined the offer.

Having found no takers for the plant, the British appointed Heinrich Nordhoff director of the plant. Before the war, Nordhoff had been an executive with Opel, a General Motors subsidiary. Nordhoff didn't think much of the VW car, but he needed a job, and his family was hungry. On New Year's Day 1948, he literally moved into the factory, sleeping on a cot next to his desk.

Because Nordhoff had no directors, stockholders, or bank officers looking over his shoulder, he was able to do as he saw fit. He began meeting regularly with his workers to inspire them toward higher levels of productivity and quality and solicit ideas toward his goal of reducing production time per car from four hundred human hours to one hundred.

All profits he plowed back into the facilities and equipment, but it became clear that the struggling company would need a larger market than postwar Germany to survive and grow. Because much of Europe was still in ruins, Nordhoff decided to go where the money was: the United States. On January 8, 1949, he shipped two VW Beetles to his only international distributor, Ben Pon in the Netherlands, with the assignment to go and conquer the Americas.

Pon was a great car dealer. He had to be, selling German cars in the Netherlands, where residual bitterness toward Germany was still powerful. Pon took one of the Beetles to the United States. The Bug got only a little publicity, much of it negative (newspapers referred to it as "Hitler's car"). U.S. auto dealers refused to take it seriously. Finally, Pon sold his model for $800 to pay his travel costs. He returned to Holland, defeated.

It was just a temporary defeat. American soldiers stationed in Europe had discovered how good the cheap little cars were and began bringing them back to this country. Their word-of-mouth praise and a write-up in *Consumer Reports* stimulated a modest demand and a growing network of dealerships. In 1950, 330 VWs sold in America; in 1955, 30,000; in 1957, 79,000.

Nordhoff felt vindicated in deciding not to restyle the ugly little car. "The only decision I am really proud of," he said years later, "is that I refused to change Porsche's design. It's hard to remain the same. You can always sell cars by being new. But we chose a different course." That course was concentrating on improving the engineering of the car and creating a service network so that VW owners would always be close to a well-stocked, competent mechanic.

All this stood in stark contrast to the road traveled by American manufacturers. This was, after all, the era of planned obsolescence, of fins, chrome, and outlandish doodads of almost every sort, of bigger and bigger "jukeboxes on wheels." Detroit didn't know what to make of VW's success. It was the opposite of what they believed consumers wanted. Henry Ford II sneered at it as "a little shitbox" lacking style, power, size, comfort, and status.

The VW cost only $1,280 in 1956. American executives were shaken to find that the people buying them weren't the poor (whom American car companies didn't consider a significant market anyway). VW customers were generally people who could afford more expensive cars but who liked the VWs no-frills design and good engineering. "The Volkswagen sells because it is, more than anything else, an honest car," noted Arthur Railton in *Popular Mechanics* in 1956. He went on:

It doesn't pretend to be anything it is not. Being an honest piece of machinery, it is one the owner can be proud of. Wherever he looks, he sees honest design and workmanship. There are no places where parts don't fit, where paint is thin, where the trim is shoddy. There are no body rattles, no water leaks. Neither, of course, is there overstuff, false luxury either. There is nothing about the car that is not sincere. One cannot imagine, for instance, a Volkswagen with a fake air scoop or tail fins to make it look like an airplane in flight.

The implied rebuke of Detroit business-as-usual by VW purchasers was not completely lost on American automakers. Feeling pressured to respond, even as its executives grumbled about those damned "gray flannel nonconformists," GM came out with what it considered a comparable car in 1959 and called it the Corvair. The problem is that they thought the success of VW had to do solely with its price, which was, at best, only half right. They cut costs on the Corvair by scrimping on key parts like stabilizer bars to keep the car from skidding out of control on corners. Possibly the worst American car ever, the Corvair inspired Ralph Nader to write his bestseller *Unsafe at Any Speed* and spawned hundreds of product liability lawsuits.

The VW Bug and van, virtually unchanged year after year and bolstered by a brilliant, honest, low-key advertising campaign, thrived for more than a decade. Detroit's refusal or inability to respond in a meaningful way to the VW challenge opened the door to other low-cost quality imports, culminating in the near take-over of the American car market by the Japanese in the 1980s.

Kellogg's Flaky Beginnings

Mucus-free and yeast-free diets? Megavitamins? Colon cleansing? Macrobiotics? If you think today's food faddists are eccentric, you should have been around during the last half of the nineteenth century. There were hundreds of regimens, each as crazy as the next.

One popular health guru of the time was Sylvester Graham, who inspired the cracker that still bears his name. He had a fanatical belief in the benefits of fresh-air exercise in all weather, whole-grain foods, and complete sexual abstinence to retain "vital bodily fluids." He believed that whole grains with bland flavorings suppressed sexual desire (health faddists take note!) and that, conversely, meat, salt, and spices were aphrodisiacs.

A disciple named James Caleb Jackson took Graham's ideas a few steps further, adding hydrotherapy—water applied to the body in the form of showers, tub baths, wet-packs, and lots of "irrigations" in all the various body cavities. Jackson developed a baked wafer of graham flour and water, which he broke into pieces and called Granula. It was America's first cold breakfast cereal. Unfortunately, it was so dry and tasteless that he couldn't get very many people to eat it.

One of the people who did eat Granula was Ellen Harmon White, founder and head prophet of the Seventh Day Adventist Church. In 1855, she and her husband convinced her entire New England congregation to stage a mass emigration to western Michigan, where she established the world headquarters of her apocalyptic religious movement, and wrote books about diet and the evils of sex. Eleven years later, she decided the world needed a health spa that would give it a taste of her medicine. She opened the Western Health Reform Institute in Battle Creek, near Adventist headquarters.

Seventh Day Adventist John Harvey Kellogg was a young school teacher in Ypsilanti, sixty miles away. White met him and apparently like the cut of his jib, because she offered to pay his tuition to Dr. Russell Trall's Hygeio-Therapeutic College in Florence Heights, New Jersey. A few years later, in 1876, the twenty-four-year-old "Dr." Kellogg returned to Michigan to become the superintendent of the sanitarium. In a case of nepotism that he would live to regret, he hired his younger brother, William Keith Kellogg, as chief clerk. William would become embittered over the years as older brother John bullied him, took him for granted, and tried to hog full credit for mutual discoveries. Years later, Will would obtain satisfaction.

Like White, John Kellogg was a believer in health food and complete sexual abstinence. He spent his honeymoon writing a tract against the evils of sex called *Plain Facts for Old and Young*. In it, he wrote that "that reproductive act is the most exhausting of all vital acts. Its effects upon the undeveloped person is to retard growth, weaken the constitution, and dwarf the intellect." Kellogg's marriage was apparently never consummated, which he believed made his wife very grateful. He wrote, "I should say that the majority of women, happily for them and for society, are not very much troubled with sexual feelings of any kind."

After much research, Kellogg decided that certain foods were especially good at suppressing desire. First, he recommended zwieback to patients—until one broke her dentures on it and demanded ten dollars to fix them. This prompted the notoriously tight-fisted doctor to begin looking for an alternative.

Kellogg tried to improve on Jackson's Granula. He and Will came up with something he called Granola—meal cakes made of wheat, corn, and oats that they ground up and served in bowls. But it was nearly as unappetizing and hard as Granula, so the brothers went back to the grain grinder to try again.

In 1885, a dream, John claimed, showed him the way to make cereals into light and crispy flakes. Divinely inspired or not, his first attempts were failures. The two brothers tried soaking wheat kernels and forcing them between steel rollers. The kernels were not flattening enough, so they began boiling them for longer and longer periods, trying to soften them enough to make a thin, flat, easily chewed flake. But even an hour of boiling wasn't enough.

One night they boiled a batch and then some emergency came up. They left the kernels soaking and didn't come back to them for a day or two. The kernels had gotten moldy, but they decided to run them through the rollers anyway. It turned out that the extra soaking was just what the doctor ordered, resulting in very thin flakes that roasted up nicely, each individual kernel becoming a well-formed, albeit moldy, flake. After experimentation, they discovered that soaking the wheat in a tin container suppressed the moldiness. They started rolling out wheat flakes.

John began taking the perfectly formed flakes and crumbling them into little pieces. It took Will some time to convince his brother that leaving the flakes whole was a better idea. A bigger problem, of course, was that nobody wanted to eat the wheat flakes because they tasted like sawdust.

Finally, in 1902, the brothers came up with a recipe that was a real crowd pleaser: corn flakes that they flavored with barley malt. Realizing that the flakes had commercial possibilities, the brothers set up a corporation, the Battle Creek Toasted Corn Flake Company, which they completely separated from the sanitarium. In their first year, they sold 100,000 pounds of corn flakes.

Along with success, they ran into problems. First of all, Sister White was furious that the Kellogg brothers had desecrated her divine institution with commercialism—and that she wasn't even getting a cut. Also, competitors and imitators began jumping onto the bandwagon (the company later changed its name to Kellogg's to distinguish it from its hundreds of imitators).

Worst of all, William Kellogg added sugar to the flakes to make them more palatable. When John Kellogg found out, he was livid. He believed that sugar would reverse the cereal's sex-suppressing effects. Will countered that sugar was necessary if they wanted people to eat the stuff. Things quickly worsened between the two brothers, culminating in a series of suits and countersuits over who owned the rights to the process, who had the rights to the Kellogg's name, and so on. Will left the sanitarium and became the cereal company's full-time president (with Dr. John retaining shares in the company).

William eventually won the lawsuits and took full control of the Kellogg's Corn Flake Company. The brothers met only a few times after. They never reconciled.

The Kellogg Company became a huge success, in part because of William's innovative advertising, promotion, giveaways, and sponsorships. One ad, considered positively risqué at the time, told women to wink at their grocers and see what they got (in most cases, by prearrangement with the company, a free sample box of Corn Flakes). It was the first cereal company to aim advertising directly toward children, knowing that they had a disproportionate power over cereal purchases in a household.

Both Will and John lived to the age of ninety-one. Will was involved in the cereal company almost to the end. John continued to preach his gospel. Even though medical findings soundly disproved most of his theories, he never abandoned them. He argued to the end that sexual activity in general sapped health and strength and in particular that masturbation caused pimples, blindness, and even death. Not surprisingly, he and his wife Ellen had no children, but they adopted and fostered forty-two children over the years. In later years, his wife became a virtual recluse while Dr. Kellogg walked the hospital grounds in all-white clothes, carrying a white cockatoo on his shoulder.

How the Energizer Bunny Keeps Its Hops Up

Did you know that the Eveready battery line is the oldest in existence? In 1896, the National Carbon Company produced the first commercially marketed dry-cell battery. Two years later, the American Electric Novelty and Manufacturing Corporation produced a novelty flashlight and called it the Eveready. When the two companies merged and became the Union Carbide Corporation, they expanded the Eveready name to the battery line as well.

Years later, Union Carbide decided to market a line of alkaline batteries. Union Carbide decided that the alkaline batteries needed to be differentiated from its line of normal batteries, so it downplayed the Eveready name and came up with a new one, the Energizer. But Union Carbide's advertising was uninspired, bordering on awful: In one commercial, tough guy actor Robert Conrad dared us to commit assault on a battery by knocking it off his shoulder; in another, Olympic star Mary Lou Retton compared her high-energy routines to high-energy Energizers.

In 1986, cereal and pet food company Ralston-Purina bought the Eveready line from Union Carbide. Ralston had a good reputation for marketing its products well. On the other hand, it never tried to sell a battery before. It made a huge mistake.

Its name was Jocko. If the ads with Conrad and Retton were mediocre, Jocko's were horrible. He was a loud, uncouth Australian wrestler whose commercials were a big hit Down Under. But in the United States, Jocko grated on everybody's nerves. The company received a dozen hate letters a day. Sales started dropping. Eveready stuck with Jocko for a year, even ludicrously trying to soften his obnoxious image with a sweater and easy chair, but it was a disaster.

Meanwhile, Duracell started a line of commercials that implied that its alkaline lasted longer than that of its main competitor, Eveready. A viewer had to pay close attention to understand that they were comparing Duracell with their own "ordinary" (carbon-zinc) batteries, not with other brands of alkalines. The commercial featured a group of battery-operated toys, each of them grinding to a stop until only the Duracell toy was still running.

Energizer decided to hit back. Their ad agency, DDB Needham, set up a battalion of stupid-looking mechanical bunnies playing cymbals, resembling those in the Duracell ads. But the demonstration is interrupted by the ultracool pink Energizer bunny wearing shades and playing a marching-band bass drum. The voice-over complains that Duracell had "never even invited us to your party."

It was an attention-getting spot, but what to do next resulted in "creative differences" between the agency and client. "We said, 'We think there's a campaign idea here. Let's do more of these,'" Eveready CEO J. Patrick Mulcahy told *Advertising Age.* "But Needham said, 'We don't think so. We don't think we can campaign this out. We think it's a one-shot deal, a limited tactical vehicle. We should put it on the air for a while and then go back to something else.'"

The client, of course, is always right. Eveready went shopping for a new agency. In February 1989, they found Chiat/Day/Mojo, which came up with the electrifying jolt Eveready was looking for. "We kind of started the way we always do, by saying 'Let's assume people don't like advertising, and they have the means to zap us with their remote control,'" said

C/D/M vice president/associate creative director Dick Sittig in an interview in *AdWeek*. "Given that, what are you going to do to grab people's attention for thirty seconds? We decided that since the battery business is kind of a low-interest category, we'd have to do something pretty out there to get people's attention. The main idea is 'How do you demonstrate long-lasting batteries?' Our notion was that you couldn't do it in just one thirty-second spot, so that's where we came up with our idea."

C/D/M decided to begin with the spot that Needham had done, but with a different ending. In the new commercial, the bunny runs amok and escapes from the studio. "It was just a simple idea based around the fact that the Energizer keeps going and going," said C/D/M CEO Bob Kuperman. "So it became the unstoppable bunny. And we thought not only will it escape from the commercial that we had done for it, but it would continue going through other commercials for other products. From there we decided to actually use the other commercial forms that we've all grown up with. The key was to make them believable and have people immediately see them as part of the real world of commercials. It had to be instantly recognizable as a coffee or nasal spray commercial."

C/D/M did extensive research on different types of commercials in order to stay true to the genre of each. Staff members found the components of each type of commercial that made them unique and distinctive: a certain editing rhythm, type of actor, copy and delivery style, lighting, film versus video, and so on. The hard part for the directors, they discovered, was trying to exactly emulate the style they were making fun of and not add any of their own individual stylistic flourishes.

The cleverness of the approach got a lot of positive attention from the press and people sitting at home on their couches. And there was another element as well: "People would rather not see those commercials anyway," said Sittig. "That's what makes the bunny a hero. If he interrupts your favorite commercial, you don't like him. But if he interrupts something you don't like, he's a hero."